Other AMACOM Books by Michael Thomsett

The Landlord's Financial Tool Kit, (AMACOM, 2005)

The Little Black Book of Project Management, 2/e, (AMACOM, 2002)

The Real Estate Investor's Pocket Calculator, (AMACOM, 2006)

ANNUAL REPORTS 101

Michael C. Thomsett

AMACOM

American Management Association
New York • Atlanta • Brussels • Chicago • Mexico City • San Francisco
Shanghai • Tokyo • Toronto • Washington, D.C.

Special discounts on bulk quantities of AMACOM books are available to corporations, professional associations, and other organizations. For details, contact Special Sales Department, AMACOM, a division of American Management Association, 1601 Broadway, New York, NY 10019.
Tel.: 212-903-8316.   Fax: 212-903-8083.
Web site: www.amacombooks.org

This publication is designed to provide accurate and authoritative information in regard to the subject matter covered. It is sold with the understanding that the publisher is not engaged in rendering legal, accounting, or other professional service. If legal advice or other expert assistance is required, the services of a competent professional person should be sought.

Library of Congress Cataloging-in-Publication Data

Thomsett, Michael C.
    Annual reports 101 : what the numbers and the fine print can reveal about the true health of a company / Michael C. Thomsett.
        p.   cm.
    Includes bibliographical references and index.
    ISBN-13: 978-0-8144-7367-2
    ISBN-10: 0-8144-7367-9
    1. Corporation reports—Evaluation—Handbooks, manuals, etc.   I. Title.

HG4028.B2T47   2007
332.63'2042—dc22
                                                                    2006017174

Printing number

10   9   8   7   6   5   4   3   2   1

CONTENTS

ANNUAL
REPORTS
101

TRANSPARENCY

FACT OR FICTION?

Anyone who has seen a corporate annual report (or a quarterly report, or financial statements by themselves) knows how difficult it is to extract meaningful and useful information from it. There is a wide communications gap between the worlds of compliance and disclosure. The legal aspects of annual reports may comply with the law and at the same time "disclose" facts—but only in a highly technical manner. What is missing for the average stockholder is clear, useful disclosures that tell you what is going on in the company. You probably have great difficulty knowing what to believe about a company based on the slick, expensively produced annual report—because it is a public relations tool and is not intended to *inform* you so much as to sway your opinion.

In many respects, the annual report is a troubling document because it mixes factual financial results with public relations information. This means that when you read an annual report, you need to be able to distinguish between these two widely varying and conflicting forms of information. To make informed decisions about whether to buy stock in a company (or to sell stock if you already own it), you need to be able to quantify the information you receive. This is a difficult task.

In order to achieve this, you have to discount some types of information, such as information that clearly is aimed at promoting the company and its stock. You may also have to discount information that attempts to interpret the financial report if, in fact, you apply tests that contradict those interpretations. For example, you may apply basic fundamental tests to the financial information to compare and judge the company's capital strength, profitability, and growth potential—whether these key factors are highlighted in the material that the company chooses to show you or not.

This is not easy. If you look back to a few decades ago, you'll find that annual reports were fairly thin documents. The financial statements were accompanied by footnotes, opinions of auditors, and various narrative sections. These included a letter from the chairman to the stockholders and a summary of the markets and operations of the company. Today, disclosures are more extensive, and footnotes often are quite complex. The annual report may easily run over 100 pages, and many of the sections, especially the footnotes, are highly technical and difficult to understand. This is not especially useful to a nonaccountant who is interested in finding straightforward answers to relatively simple questions. These questions include the all-important one: Is the company a viable long-term investment, and is its capital strength improving or declining?

Today, this question is not easily answered using the annual report. The answers are there, but they are not easy to find. This situation has been brought about partially by the increased disclosure requirements imposed by federal and state regulation, especially following the period of widespread and expensive corporate corruption such as that seen at Enron and WorldCom. It has become typical that footnotes and annual reports today are less informative for you as a would-be investor, and more likely to satisfy a legal disclosure requirement. This problem is augmented by the fact that there are two tiers of people who use annual reports. The first is the individual investor, who has to struggle to make sense out of the volume of technical information; the second is the accountants, executives, analysts, and regulators, who understand the complexities of finance and, unfortunately, may be completely unaware of the gap between themselves and the rest of the investing world.

The highly technical accounting and analytical language and footnotes in the annual report are often of very little use to anyone who has not had an accounting education. For this reason, you cannot simply rely on the disclosures in the annual report. First of all, they are often difficult to interpret and to understand. Second, transparency in a real sense does not exist in the annual report. The footnotes are intended to satisfy the legal form of transparency, not to provide the real-world disclosures that you need and want. You need sound, nontechnical information that will allow you to judge the corporation as a potential investment, and because corporate transparency has not yet been realized, you need to peel away the public relations layers and discover the truly important data underneath. Until corporations take steps to create transparency, you'll need to employ various techniques to find the information to make informed decisions.

This book is designed to provide you with these all-important tools. It begins with a nontechnical explanation of how accounting rules work and what the problems are within the accounting culture. An examination of the basic financial statements follows, including a review of the essential ratios that you need in order to understand the numbers themselves.

The book also examines what the annual report does not reveal at first glance and provides you with the tools to dig deeper. This includes what the footnotes reveal, enabling you to find real disclosures and to identify the red flags that you can find on your own. The book also breaks down the structure of the annual report as a public relations document and explains how and why that works more to promote and market the company than to disclose useful information to you and to enable you to interpret and make use of the information that is there.

The auditing role is also explained in the context of how the accounting culture deals with its own conflicts of interest. Because auditing firms are paid to perform both audits and other nonaudit work, the accounting mentality complicates the reporting and disclosure functions of the annual report. In Chapter 9, you will find the six methods used to manipulate numbers and to distort rather than reveal. These accounting shell games are commonly used and often may be disguised in such a way that the accountant and the corporate executive are in compliance with the law, while also distorting the information that you receive. This information helps you to interpret the financial aspects of the annual report, in the statements and the footnotes.

The purpose of this book is to simplify the annual report. That may

seem a daunting task, but it does not have to be, if you develop a short
list of essential points to check. Another purpose is to provide you with
the means to understand what you have before you with the annual report, without requiring you to acquire an accounting education along
the way.

CHAPTER 1

THE ACCOUNTING DILEMMA

THE GAP IN GAAP

Ownership of stock is widespread as a result of the expansion of retirement funds. In addition to direct ownership of stocks, investors become stockholders through the purchase of mutual fund shares, government-sponsored programs, and corporate retirement funds. Among employees between the ages of 21 and 64, about 57 percent participate in employer-based retirement plans. The staggering sum of $11.4 trillion is invested through a variety of organized retirement programs, including nearly $5 trillion in 401(k), IRA, and Keogh accounts.[1]

When you add to this the money invested in stocks through mutual funds and stocks purchased directly, you realize that *most* working people are involved in the stock market. So the study of annual reports should not be limited to mutual fund managers or wealthy individuals. The way companies report their earnings affects most people. The major sources of information about companies—the financial statements—are found in the annual report to stockholders. But there are problems.

When you study a company's annual report, you may begin with a series of assumptions—the financial statements are complete, accurate, and fair, for example. You may also assume that all disclosures have been made adequately.

These assumptions are not always realistic. In fact, accounting is a passive activity. Even when all of the information is presented to you in the annual report, an audit does nothing to highlight problems or to point out weaknesses; an auditor's job is merely to ensure that the statements conform to the rules. Unfortunately for the average investor, this assurance is of little value or help. Companies and their auditors are under a lot of pressure to meet analysts' projections concerning revenues and earnings; and if the results fall short, executives' jobs may be on the line. Executives' compensation, analysts' reputations, and auditors' accounts are all at risk when a company's results don't meet expectations. It is especially perverse that a *prediction* becomes the standard against which actual results are measured, but that is how things are done. Wall Street places great importance on predictions, even though the clarity and reliability of the fundamental reporting should be the standard.

The problem begins with the culture and workings of the accounting industry itself. Most people don't know exactly how the accounting industry sets its own rules, and that's because there is no single, central organization that coordinates those rules. Rather, the industry operates under a collection of precepts that come from many different places. The system known as GAAP (Generally Accepted Accounting Principles) is made up of a complex series of opinions, rules, and publications.

Key point: The GAAP system is not centrally controlled, but consists of a series of publications and studies in many places.

You may believe that there is a single, universally agreed-upon set of rules and standards for accountants. There is not. Decisions about when and how to recognize revenue, costs, and expenses can be very complex, and accountants often disagree with one another on how a particular transaction should be treated.

This affects the way in which annual reports are prepared. The financial statements and related footnotes are the result of a corporation's financial decisions. These are made during the year in the company's accounting departments, reviewed and approved by vice presidents and the CFO (chief financial officer), and then reviewed by an internal auditing department. Finally, an outside accounting firm enters the picture to examine the books and records and to render an opinion through the independent audit process.

This independent audit is not entirely independent. The same firm that conducts the audit often also performs a number of nonaudit services for the corporation—consultation on a range of legal, accounting, bookkeeping, computer, and systems matters, depending on the company's needs and the firm's expertise. The Sarbanes-Oxley Act of 2002 was supposed to fix this problem, but it has had very little effect. So the audit, although performed by an "outsider," is not necessarily objective in every sense. Realistically, an auditing firm whose client pays it millions of dollars per year in various fees will not want to get into major disagreements with that client's management. This is where GAAP comes into play.

The fact that auditing firms carry out a lot of nonaudit work is a huge issue within the accounting industry. It has led to problems in the past. At the onset of the infamous corporate scandals, for example, the Securities and Exchange Commission (SEC) was conducting more than 250 investigations involving accounting inaccuracies or nondisclosures.[2] Throughout the 2001–2002 period, many additional accounting problems became public knowledge, contradicting the long-held belief that the audited statements were the last word and could be relied upon by everyone.

▲ THE AUDITING CULTURE

The GAAP system is so broad and complex that justification for a number of possible outcomes can be found within the rules and opinions. A company with a very conservative accounting policy may find support for conservative decisions within GAAP, and one with a more aggressive attitude, in which income is maximized and the rules are bent, can also find justification. This is not to say that the accounting industry is disingenuous or dishonest; but the issues are so highly technical that there is often more than one clear, simple answer.

The auditing firm gets involved in examining the books and records of the company after the end of the fiscal year. (In larger corporations, quarterly reviews are also performed to reduce the year-end workload, and in some cases, an audit team operates within the corporation year-round.) The audit process is far different from what many nonaccountants believe, as is the conclusiveness of the outcome.

Key point: There is no one right answer in the audit. There are so many possible interpretations under the GAAP system that many conclusions can be drawn.

When you read an auditor's opinion letter stating that the books and records are an accurate and consistent representation of the year's transactions, you might tend to think that this assurance is ironclad. History has shown, though, that it is not. Throughout the 1990s, numerous lawsuits were filed by shareholders and state securities agencies against many of the most prestigious auditing firms, and the majority ended in sizable settlements paid. The problems experienced by the late Arthur Andersen & Co., auditor for Enron, are well-known. However, the other major large national auditing firms were also involved in corporate scandals. Based on the numerous lawsuits filed against auditing firms during the first years of the new century, accounting opinions cannot be depended upon as completely as investors believed in the past. Although large numbers of these lawsuits were filed due to accounting irregularities, one unfortunate consequence is the added complexity in annual reports.

This problem has ramifications for everyone who is reviewing annual financial statements. How do you know whether you can trust the auditor's opinion? Even with the passage of new, tough, federal legislation requiring that auditors eliminate conflicts of interest, you cannot rely completely on the audited statements. Under this new law (the Sarbanes-Oxley Act of 2002), auditors cannot confer directly with a corporation's executives. Auditing firms are selected and hired by an audit committee rather than by financial officers, and any disputes that arise during the audit have to be settled between the audit team and the audit committee.

These are all excellent steps toward removing obvious conflicts of interest, and the situation today is much better than it was in the past. But as a wise investor, you should proceed cautiously and view the annual report with skepticism. Remember, in the accounting culture, there is a lack of understanding of what you, as an investor, need and want to see. Even the most diligent auditor who strives to present the final financial statements as honestly as possible exists within that culture. The auditor is likely to communicate well with the financial officers on the audit committee, but not so well with outsiders. Any nonaccountant will have difficulty grasping the highly technical accounting decisions that auditors have to contend with. Even so, when all of the technical issues are peeled away, you find that the questions are not as complex as accountants treat them, and that the average nonaccountant can grasp the importance of the underlying facts.

The gap between disclosure and transparency is a large one. The accounting culture understands *disclosure* quite well. Accountants know how to make sure that all of the relevant facts are documented in footnotes. The problem, though, is that this disclosure process is far from a *transparent* one. The typical investor reading the footnotes to a financial statement will have as much difficulty understanding the explanations as he would have reading the text of a law.

Key point: It is easy to confuse disclosure and transparency. In fact, the two concepts operate quite differently in the annual report.

For example, the Motorola annual report (www.motorola.com), which covers 148 pages, includes this explanation of how and when it records revenues in its books:

Revenue Recognition: The company recognizes revenue for product sales when title transfers, the risks and rewards of ownership have been transferred to the customer, the fee is fixed and determinable, and collection of the related receivable is probable, which is generally at the time of shipment. Accruals are established, with the related reduction to revenue, for allowances for discounts and price protection, product returns and incentive programs for distributors and end customers related to these sales based on actual historical exposure at the time the related revenues are recognized.[3]

In fairness to Motorola, this is not an atypical explanation. However, it illustrates the problem: The method of disclosure is not user-friendly by any means. The statement (which often goes into even more technical detail than the example given) basically discloses that revenue is normally booked when goods are shipped, and that any discounts or other offsets are booked at the same time. This is a rather simple idea, and, in the spirit of transparency, it would be easy for a company to simplify its explanations. But with the large number of state securities lawsuits and investor lawsuits against corporations, the annual report—that once-simple document that summarizes what happened during the past year—has become an essential *legal* document designed to disclose the legal points that the corporation needs to make. The annual report today is designed to protect the corporate executives and the auditing firm from lawsuits, not to give essential information to investors.

Because GAAP offers great flexibility in determining how and when to recognize transactions, the auditor's opinion is not absolute; it only ensures that the report fits within the rules. It does *not* ensure that it is the best or even the most accurate reflection of operations.

Key point: The auditor's report only ensures that the company's books conform to the standards within the GAAP system. It does not certify that the decisions made by the company are the *most* accurate or the *only* possible interpretation.

▲ THE GAAP SYSTEM—FLEXIBILITY IN THE RULES

The creation of new systems is never easy. This is nowhere more true than in the massive and complicated GAAP system.

GAAP consists of a series of rules, conventions, opinions, and standards developed by numerous agencies. The SEC recognizes the Financial Accounting Standards Board (FASB) as the authoritative body for setting financial accounting and reporting standards. The AICPA agrees, so the FASB has the central authority to make rulings.[4]

Even so, the process is time-consuming and complex because the

FASB receives information and opinions from many sources. The organization of the FASB itself is complex. The Financial Accounting Standards Advisory Committee (FASAC) consults with the FASB on technical questions and organizes task forces to address those questions. The Financial Accounting Foundation (FAF) selects members of the FASB and the advisory committee.[5]

The organization, in other words, is a committee that is appointed and overseen by other committees. Perhaps this complex structure is necessary for a board that is responsible for such a broad array of standards; however, one of the troubling aspects of the corporate scandals that came to light in 2002 is that even with careful definition of accounting standards, it was all too easy for many corporations to make use of the GAAP rules to manipulate the books—at times with their auditing firms' compliance or with its passive acceptance and silence.

> **Key point:** Many people think of GAAP as a single entity. In fact, it is overseen by a committee supervising a series of other committees.

While the whole GAAP structure is likely to be strengthened through various reforms and new laws, it remains complex, providing great latitude in the interpretation of facts. Even the name makes this point. *Generally accepted* may indicate that the rulings are agreed upon by most experts in the field. However, many GAAP rulings are not accepted widely, and many others contradict separate rulings. The GAAP system is far from a central clearinghouse for ultimate decisions. It is not a court, nor does it function as an arbitrator of disputes. The FASB publishes rules and opinions, but GAAP itself is not a tangible, single entity.

> **Key point:** The GAAP system is a complex array of many agencies, boards, committees, and publications. The system provides no easy answers—only a series of opinions and often contradictory rules.

GAAP involves what is called a "hierarchy of authority" system, with a total of five distinct categories.

The higher the level of authority, the greater the weight given to a specific rule.[6] Category A, the highest level, consists of Statements of Financial Accounting Standards, FASB Interpretations, Accounting Principles Board Opinions, and Accounting Research Bulletins. Category B includes FASB Technical Bulletins, AICPA Industry Audit and Accounting Guidelines, and AICPA Statements of Position. Category C includes so-called consensus positions of the FASB Emerging Issues Task Force and the AICPA Accounting Standards Executive Committee. Category D includes AICPA Accounting Interpretations, FASB Staff Implementation Guides, and what the AICPA calls "practices that are widely recognized and prevalent with generally or in the industry."[7] Finally, Category E is an "all other" classification. It includes many publications of the FASB, the AICPA, and other agencies, as well as accounting textbooks and articles.

If it seems as though the industry itself is constantly struggling with its own technical issues, there is a reason for this. Accounting is complex, and new issues emerge constantly. Just like the law, GAAP is a dynamic institution with no specific identity or home, but a loosely constructed grouping of committees, boards, and publications. The very scope of the rules makes it possible to find contradictory opinions in virtually any situation.

The complex hierarchy that constitutes GAAP is summarized in Table 1.1.

Even with the far-reaching and complex GAAP system, history shows that no level of rule setting can anticipate or prevent all forms of abuse. To some degree, it is the very complexity of GAAP that enables corporations and auditing firms to interpret outcomes so liberally. Reform is needed not only with regard to corporate disclosure and auditing conflicts of interest, but also in the methods employed by FASB, the AICPA, and the many other agencies and committees involved with the GAAP system. How that is to be accomplished is a complex question.

For investors, the lesson is an important one: The system does not provide a single, clear authority for accounting decisions. Despite the efforts to create an orderly and consistent system, the result is uncertainty, great interpretative latitude, and the opportunity for abuse—not necessarily through any intentional design, but simply as a consequence of the complex questions that arise in accounting and auditing work.

TABLE 1.1   GAAP HIERARCHY.

A —Statements of Financial Accounting Standards (FASB)
—FASB Interpretations (FASB)
—Accounting Principles Board Opinions (APB)
—Accounting Research Bulletins (AICPA)

  B —Technical Bulletins (FASB)
—Industry Audit and Accounting Guides (AICPA)
—Statements of Position (AICPA)

    C —Consensus position, Emerging Issues Task Force (FASB)
—Accounting Standards Executive Committee practice bulletins (AICPA)

      D —Accounting Interpretations (AICPA)
—Staff Implementation Guides (FASB)
—Industry practices

        E —Statements of Financial Accounting Concepts (FASB)
—Federal Accounting Standards Advisory Board Statements, Interpretations, and Technical Bulletins (FASAB)
—Issue papers (AICPA)
—Technical practice aids (AICPA)
—Government Accounting Standards Board Statements (GASB)
—International Accounting Standards Board Statements (IASB)
—Pronouncements of other professional associations and regulatory agencies; and accounting textbooks and articles

---

These problems are reflected in the annual report—not only in the design and disclosure of financial information, but also in its complexity. There is a reason that annual reports are difficult to interpret: They are the products of GAAP complexity and the legal exposure of corporations and auditors. In this environment, real transparency is an elusive goal.

▲ THE SARBANES-OXLEY ACT AND FINANCIAL REPORTING

The annual report is prepared from several points of view: Financial, public relations, and legal considerations are mixed together in the document. In 2002, Congress passed a law called the Sarbanes-Oxley Act (SOX) that was designed to do away with the abuses of the auditing and accounting processes and to remove conflicts of interest from the process.

Historically, accounting firms that perform external audits have always had a conflict of interest because they could not be completely objective. The services that these firms provided to their corporate clients included many things beyond audit work; in fact, in the past, more than half of all accounting firm revenues came from nonaudit functions (legal, systems, internal controls, and other work).

So if an auditing firm disagrees with corporate management about an accounting decision, what happens? Can the audit firm afford to lose a big client? Many large corporations pay millions of dollars per year in audit and nonaudit consulting fees, so senior auditors who interact with corporations are keenly aware of what is on the line. In fact, auditors' performance is normally measured by the revenues generated by their clients. Thus, if a senior auditor loses a big account over an accounting disagreement, it could spell the end of that person's career. This is a lot of pressure.

That describes the way things were for many years. Corporations consolidated their grip on their "external" auditing firms by hiring senior auditors away from their firms and giving them jobs as CFO with big salaries and bonuses. The ever-present threat of losing the account also made it difficult for senior auditors to perform their primary role: the objective analysis of the accounting records. The stockholder, the ultimate client of the external audit, was cut out of the loop.

Key point: The inherent conflict of interest among accounting firms comes from their performing so-called independent audits while also providing a broad range of consulting services to the same client.

Sarbanes-Oxley fixed the more glaring conflicts of interest with several provisions, including the following:

1. *The act set up an oversight board.* The Public Company Accounting Oversight Board was set up under SOX specifically to monitor and regu-

late auditing firms. The board is supervised by the Securities and Exchange Commission (SEC). It is empowered to establish auditing standards, inspect accounting firms that conduct audits of publicly listed companies, investigate violations, and impose sanctions.

The very fact that the government saw fit to set up an oversight board is a condemnation of the accounting industry. Like many other industries (medical, legal, investment, and insurance, to name a few), the accounting industry had always regulated itself through national and state accounting associations. But it became clear by 2002 that the accounting industry could not be trusted to reform itself, so the government stepped in. The crux of the problem (the complexity of GAAP itself) was largely behind the decision to enable the board to set accounting standards. A criticism of the FASB was included in the act's intention. The criticism observed, "By making rules complex and detailed, [the FASB's approach] invites accountants to look for loopholes in the rules."[8]

2. *Services are restricted.* Auditing firms are prohibited under SOX from performing many nonaudit services for the companies that they audit. Specifically, firms can no longer perform both audit work and nine specific areas of consultation: bookkeeping; financial systems design and implementation; appraisal, valuation, and fairness opinions; actuarial services; internal audit services; management services; human resources services; broker-dealer services; and legal services.

The purpose of separating these nonaudit services from the auditing function was to ensure that auditing firms would not be placed in the position of approving internal systems that the firms themselves had designed, as well as attempting to remove the incentive to compromise on audit matters because receipts from other work had become significant. However, a few years after enactment of SOX, it appears that there has been little change. Auditing firms have either reclassified the services that they offer or spun off those services to subsidiary companies in many instances.

3. *Audit partners must rotate off accounts.* In the past, audit partners of accounting firms were so involved with their client companies that they were at those corporate offices practically full time. It became increasingly difficult for the audit partners to maintain enough distance (personally as well as professionally) to ensure objectivity. Thus, the act does not

permit any one accounting firm partner to be involved with any one company for longer than five years.

4. *Auditing firms now report to the company's audit committee.* In the past, auditing firms were hired and supervised by the CFO and/or the CEO of the company being audited. Because those executives could fire a firm, they were able to exert a lot of influence on how audits were conducted. SOX required the establishment of a committee of the board of directors called the audit committee. Auditing firms now report directly to this committee, and the committee has sole power to negotiate fees and hire or fire an auditing firm. Any disagreements in interpretations of accounting rules have to be negotiated with the committee as well. In short, the financial executives of a company cannot have contact with auditors.

5. *Auditors cannot move directly into corporate roles.* It was common practice in the past for companies to hire accountants directly from the auditing team. So a senior auditor could change roles and become CFO immediately. Under SOX, a "cooling-off period" is required. An auditing firm cannot audit a company if any member of that company's senior management worked for the auditing firm during the previous 12 months.

The conflicts of interest within accounting firms were such a large problem in the past that SOX left the door open to possibly requiring mandatory rotation of accounting firms in the future. If that provision is ever put into effect, publicly listed companies will have to change accounting firms periodically.

▲ DISCLOSURE VERSUS TRANSPARENCY

An audit—even the best, most accurate one—is limited to the numbers. This means that all disclosures are included in the financial statements and the footnotes, but beyond that, the audit provides no information. Detailed footnotes might explain the assumptions used to establish value, time transactions, or amortize an asset. But what if the capital structure of the business is deteriorating? The audit will not say anything about this.

Key point: The audit only discloses; it does *not* provide any interpretations of what the numbers mean for investors.

For example, one feature worth monitoring is capitalization. The combination of equity and long-term debt is called "total capitalization," and analysts like to track the relative value of each element over time. If debt as a percentage of total capitalization is increasing from one year to the next, this is sometimes a very negative sign for investors. The higher the long-term debt, the worse the situation. As debt grows, more and more working capital will have to be devoted to debt repayment in the future. And the greater the debt, the higher the annual interest expense. If operating profits increasingly have to go to paying interest, that reduces the cash available to pay dividends.

In an audit, the valuation of long-term debt and of equity is checked and verified. The auditor will confidently sign off on the valuation, but provides no comments about the trend in total capitalization. Even though many investors believe that the auditor's job is to highlight such problems, it is not. An analyst will do so, but you cannot rely on the external audit to point out emerging trends.

Management likes to discuss trends in its portion of the annual report. In the letter from the chairman or CEO, management discussion and analysis, and those sections devoted to explaining the various markets and products, corporate management is always happy to highlight various trends. But because management is motivated to highlight the positive, it is unlikely that these sections will provide any mention of emerging *negative* trends.

Key point: Don't depend too heavily on management's own interpretation of trends. It is not likely that negative trends will be given the same amount of ink as positive ones, and even the negative trends are likely to be cast in a positive light.

You are left with a document that combines financial facts with public relations messages. To the extent that management does interpret its own numbers, it will tend to ignore any adverse information and emphasize the positive. In fact, when explaining negative information, management tends to put a positive spin on it. When sales and profits are down, management might explain that "during this period of consolidation, we made many difficult decisions and redefined our marketing priorities." You are not likely to find an annual report in which the CEO explains that "we had a poor year because we didn't do a good job of anticipating the market or competing effectively."

A lot of attention has been paid to this very problem in recent years. There has been a long-established trend in which annual reports are used to attract new institutional investors as well as individuals, to assure analysts that all is well, and to keep the current stockholders happy. The emerging call for *transparency* sounds like a trend toward disclosure of all the news, including an honest discussion of what it means. It also refers to a complete disclosure of everything that is important to investors, both positive and negative. In practice, corporations and auditors have a long way to go, because transparency—even though the concept has been applauded widely—will ultimately mean much more than it does today.

Realistically, you need to view the annual report as a starting point. All of the facts are there for you to interpret. But you cannot rely on management to explain the annual report completely. And you certainly cannot rely on the passive audit to go beyond the simple verification of the numbers.

Key point: The annual report is valuable as a starting point, but don't rely on the audit opinion and management's explanations alone. You need to perform your own critical analysis.

This is not to say that the annual report is useless. On the contrary, it contains the information you need to make an informed judgment. However, you need to study the financial statements and footnotes on your own in order to arrive at any conclusive and insightful results. It is a great failure of business that the communications opportunities available through published annual reports are not used to inform stockholders. Instead, corporate management tends to view the annual report from a legal and public relations perspective. In many respects, management is out of touch with stockholders, especially those without the resources or the training to perform in-depth analysis. The nonaccountant is at a great disadvantage in evaluating companies based on their annual reports, and this fact is not acknowledged by most corporations in the way they explain their own operations.

▲ PUBLIC RELATIONS VERSUS FINANCIAL SECTIONS

In reviewing the major sections of the annual report, it becomes apparent that there are two primary types of information: public relations or marketing on the one hand, and disclosure on the other. There is no single format for an annual report, although it would be desirable to institute a specific arrangement and format for information. It is very difficult for most people to make valid side-by-side comparisons because of the different formats that companies use.

For example, some companies include ten years of key financial figures; others provide only five years or only current and past year information. The "key financial figures" are not always the same, either. In performing a comparative analysis of two or more companies, you cannot simply go to the same section of each annual report and copy the numbers that you want to study. You often need to do some digging because of the inconsistencies in how annual reports are organized and in how much information is actually provided.

> **Key point:** Because there is no uniformly used format for annual reports, every company provides information in a different format. This makes company-to-company comparisons very difficult.

The following public relations sections are usually found somewhere in an annual report:

1. *Chairman or CEO's letter.* This public relations section of the annual report is an explanation by the top executive of what occurred during the past year. Even when the operations were dismal, you are rarely

going to find a frank discussion here. A positive spin can be put on anything, even increasing net losses, rising expenses, and loss of market share.
One of the more infamous corporate scandals involved the appliance
manufacturer Sunbeam, where profits were overstated over several years
as a result of accounting misrepresentations. In the 1997 annual report,
the chairman's letter called 1997 an "amazing year" and pointed to
"major initiatives to transform the Company into a leaner, more profitable company"—when, in reality, that year's results included more than
$8 billion in reduced cash flow.[9]

The letter was probably not written by the chairman or CEO, but by
a public relations employee or consultant. It would be a mistake to assume that the letter is a real communication from the executive to stockholders. At best, the CEO may approve the text before it is published; but
most of these letters are not actually drafted by the person who signs
them.

2. *Markets and product lines.* This is usually the glossiest part of the
annual report, entirely public relations in content. It may be interesting
to someone who is new to the company in the sense that it is informative,
but from the point of view of financial strength or even competitive position, this section is of no value. However, most investors will benefit
from knowing what the company sells, where its markets are, and what
prospects it has for the future.

Numerous other sections of the annual report involve financial matters, although most of these are passive in nature, meaning that information is provided, but it usually is not interpreted objectively. These
sections include the following:

1. *Financial statements.* This is a summary of the status and operations of the business. There are three primary statements: The balance
sheet summarizes the values of assets, liabilities, and stockholders' equity
as of the end of the fiscal year. The summary of operations (also called
the profit and loss statement or the income statement) reports on the
year's revenues, costs, expenses, and profits, and always ends on the same
date as that used for the balance sheet. Finally, the statement of cash flows
reports on where money came from and how it was spent. Subsidiary
statements are often included to summarize expenses, the details of stock-

holders' equity, or breakdowns of revenues, costs, and expenses by major segments within the operation. As with all financial sections, a major problem here is that every company uses a different format for its financial statements, with some providing more details than others. It is difficult, for example, to compare major segments and break down operations by operating units. Not every corporation provides the same level of detail.

2. *Footnotes.* Often referred to only as "notes," this is often the largest section of the annual report. Footnotes may take up 100 pages or more and are highly technical. However, nonaccountants can derive information by skimming through the notes, which provide not only disclosures but also explanations of how valuations were arrived at in many instances.

3. *Auditor's opinion letter.* This letter explains the auditor's view about the fairness and accuracy of the financial statements. If management and the auditor have disagreed about any matters that remain unresolved, the auditor's opinion will contain qualifications; read these carefully, because these disagreements may bring into question the reliability of the financial statements themselves.

4. *Summary of key financial figures.* It would be highly desirable if all corporations would provide 10 years of summarized information. Most do not. Some provide ten; others give out only five years' worth. Some of the more valuable analysis is performed by tracking key ratios or operating results over an entire decade. Many companies either are unaware of the importance of this information or don't want to publish it for the whole world to see. In addition, not every corporation provides the same level of detail. Common information includes current assets and liabilities, long-term assets and liabilities, stock price history, dividends declared and paid, P/E ratio, shareholders' equity, revenues, costs, expenses, operating profit, revenue from the sale of capital assets, and other nonrecurring sources of revenue or losses.

5. *Management discussion and analysis.* This is one of the more interesting financial sections of the annual report. Here, management explains what—in its opinion—the operating results really mean. There is an obvious bias in asking management to explain how well or how poorly it managed operations, or to attempt to explain why revenues and profits

were down. A wise outsider will look at the information provided by management with the understanding that it may be slanted to favor the executive view. At the same time, under Sarbanes-Oxley, management is held to a high standard of disclosure. Not only do the CEO and the CFO have to certify the accuracy of the company's financial statements (and doing so falsely carries both civil and criminal penalties), but they also have to ensure that their own statements in this section of the annual report are not misleading. So since 2002, when SOX was enacted, you are likely to see a far more cautious tone in this section of the annual report.

6. *Officers, directors, and addresses.* The annual report usually includes a list of the members of the board of directors and senior management. Additionally, many corporations include the address of the company's home office and the locations of major subsidiaries.

The sections of the annual report do not appear in any specific sequence or arrangement. These sections are summarized in Figure 1.2.

▲ REPORTING IN THE CORPORATE CULTURE

Anyone outside of the accounting and corporate cultures is at a disadvantage. Investors often believe that the effort put into preparing the annual

FIGURE 1.1

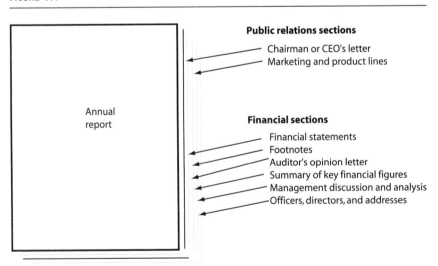

report is aimed 100 percent at disclosure and explanation. This belief—
that transparency is the primary objective of the annual report—is not
accurate. It does not reflect the attitude within the corporate world.

From the insider's point of view, there are three primary concerns
and priorities in preparing the annual report. These are:

1. *Compliance with regulatory requirements.* Foremost in the minds of
the corporate executives are the ever-present federal and state regulatory
agencies. For every listed company, this regulatory presence involves state
securities agencies and the Securities and Exchange Commission (SEC).
Regulation of listed companies and their published financial statements
is one of the primary functions of the SEC, which also enforces all provisions of SOX. Because the penalties for filing inaccurate reports can be
daunting, executives are understandably in a defensive mode when certi-
fying the reports prepared for their corporations.

Why isn't there greater transparency? The answer: Because the annual
report and its financial statements (as well as quarterly filings with the
SEC) are *compliance* documents. The oddity of the annual report is that it
combines this compliance requirement with the public relations element.
Unfortunately, the complexities of the financial report are far from transparent for most individual investors.

2. *Maintenance of holdings by large institutional investors.* The corporate mentality looks at the mix of stockholders, paying special attention
to its major source of capital, large institutional investors. These mutual
funds, pension plan administrators, and insurance companies account for
the vast majority of all holdings and trading of stocks. So it is imperative
for corporations to remain in the good graces of institutional investors,
because if those investors were to sell off their shares, it would be disas-
trous from the corporate point of view.

3. *Keeping profits (and thus the stock price) up.* Remaining in the good
graces of institutional investors is so important because it has everything
to do with keeping the stock price as high as possible. If institutional
investors began selling off large blocks of stock, the sudden oversupply
on the market would force the stock price to fall. Because many executives' annual compensation includes a large numbers of stock options,
that can translate to millions of dollars in income lost or gained. So there

is a built-in conflict of interest for corporate executives. This was one of the major factors in many of the corporate scandals that came to light in 2001 and 2002. The SOX requirement that executives have no contact with auditors is a good step toward removing this conflict; but realistically, the problem remains, even if it is not as obvious.

An equally disturbing reality is that virtually everyone in the corporate and audit environments is motivated to want profits to be as high and as consistent as possible. Investors like predictability, and corporate executives have to cater to investors. There were two levels of corporate manipulation of profits. The first was outright distortion of the numbers: booking artificial revenue, capitalizing expenses, and similar techniques. The second was the so-called sugar bowl or cookie jar accounting: techniques designed to create consistent growth in sales and profits. In exceptionally profitable years, portions of revenues were deferred to future years, creating artificial reserves, so that the long-term trends appeared more predictable than they actually were. In lower-volume years, corporations dipped into the "sugar bowl" and used some of these reserves. This is a troubling practice because it is not accurate. Year-to-year results are frequently chaotic and inconsistent. But from the corporate point of view, consistency is often so desirable that great effort is put into justifying accounting decisions that are not entirely accurate.

Unfortunately for investors, accounting rules leave room for manipulation and even for unrealistic outcomes. One thing that accounting rules do not necessarily deliver is clarity. In seeking to identify high-quality earnings and long-term growth, you cannot gain any insight from what the financial statements or footnotes tell you. It is likely that the tone of the audited statement will be more confusing than enlightening.

Accounting rules start with a few basic concepts, and these form the basis for how the reporting rules are set (and how they can be used to manipulate results). Transactions are reported on the accrual basis, which means that all revenues are reported in the period in which they are earned, even if payment is not received until later; and all costs and expenses are booked when they are incurred, even if payment isn't made until later. This accrual system is necessary in order to ensure that transactions conform to the "matching principle" (making sure that related revenue, costs, and expenses appear in the same period), but it also opens the door for abuse of the system.

The confusion is augmented by the fact that there are at least three different versions of a financial outcome. These are:

1. *The GAAP format.* This is the financial statements seen by investors and analysts—the "official" version based on interpretations of the rules. It is subjective because many transactions can be treated in different ways, and corporate accounting departments and auditors make decisions based on their reading of what is allowed.

2. *The statutory format.* The calculation of transactions under the law, and specifically what is reported for tax purposes, is not the same as the official version. For example, depreciation expense may be calculated on a vastly different basis in each version of the financial statements.

3. *The core earnings format.* Some profit and loss—specifically, any that is nonoperational and nonrecurring—is not part of the "core earnings" of the company. When a division is sold, capital assets are disposed of at a profit, or accounting assumptions are restated, nonrecurring profit or loss results. So there often is quite a difference between *operating* profit and *net* profit.

▲ CORPORATE INSIDERS: ACCOUNTING CULTURE REVISITED

The solutions to the problems with using annual report information may involve long-term changes in both the accounting and corporate cultures. These could include the following four changes:

1. *A revised point of view among auditing firms.* The accounting industry has not reformed itself. Although SOX bans auditing firms from performing both audit and specific categories of nonaudit services, auditing firms have been able to find ways around the rules. To truly remove the conflict of interest, firms would better serve their clients and the

public by making a clear distinction: Either perform only audit services for a specific client or perform everything but audit work. Since there is plenty of work to go around, it is even possible to make arrangements for this cooperatively between competing auditing firms. If firms were to split the work to be performed on a reciprocal basis, everyone would benefit. It is apparent, however, that auditing firms are not willing to enact such sweeping reform, and to date, the accounting associations have not stepped forward. The AICPA, as the country's primary accounting association, could help to make such changes occur.

2. *Corporate leadership in removing auditor conflicts.* Corporate leaders could also fix the conflict of interest problem, and quite simply. If firms used one accounting firm for their audit work and another for all other services, the entire matter could be corrected easily. Failing this, the SEC may eventually require corporations to rotate the firms it uses periodically. SOX leaves open this possibility, but the decision to force such drastic measures through legislation would be a less desirable alternative.

3. *Corporate agreement on uniform reporting standards.* The annual reports for different companies contain many of the same elements, but not in the same format. Anyone trying to make comparisons among companies will run into difficulties because there is no one standard reporting format. Corporations would contribute to real transparency by agreeing on how the annual report should be organized and the amount of information it provides. Exchanges could be helpful as well by working with listed companies and even enacting new reporting-based listing requirements.

4. *Demands for transparency from investors.* Finally, the real pressure for meaningful reform may come from investors. By demanding that corporations and accounting firms eliminate their conflicts of interest, investors could be quite influential in creating the kinds of change that would lead to real transparency. Investors can write to corporate executives, whose names can often be found on their companies' web sites, and propose such changes as a means of influencing these decisions.

The annual report contains the information, but it goes only so far. The conflict between the highly desirable theme of transparency and the preferred public relations approach used in most annual reports is a problem for virtually everyone. The preference for compliance over transparency is created both by the complexities of the law and by the self-interest of executives, whose compensation may be largely incentive-based. These are intrinsic problems not only within the investment community, but also in the business world itself. It may take several years for reform to truly take hold. The Sarbanes-Oxley Act of 2002 is a beginning of reform, but real change has to occur on a cultural level within companies and must be led by farsighted managers. That takes time.

Even with all of the problems inherent in how auditors and management work, and with the cryptic technical features of the annual report, you can find and use valuable information. Chapter 2 begins the journey by explaining how the financial statements are organized and what they reveal.

The Basic Financial Statements

What Your Mama Didn't Tell You About the Balance Sheet

Reading a financial statement is like putting together a jigsaw puzzle. All of the pieces are there, but the picture is complicated. In the annual report, the combination of the statements and footnotes is further complicated by the size of the document, the public relations sections, and the highly technical aspects of accounting. Even so, you can find and use a large amount of information without an accounting background.

The accounting profession may be seen as having rules on three different levels. The first and easiest to comprehend is the *bookkeeping system*. There are a few basic rules regarding how transactions are recorded, how they are documented, and how the audit trail is created. (The audit trail is the method used to trace transactions from original documents, such as invoices or receipts, through to the financial statements themselves.) The second is the *decisions* that accountants make, based on rules and procedures for how accountants behave and how they prepare documents for their work. For example, in determining when to recognize revenue and record it in the books, rules apply; if accountants deviate from those rules, they need to justify doing so. Let's say that revenue is usually booked when goods are shipped. This month, a new customer places an exceptionally large order, and the company invests in raw materials and production plant to fill that order. This investment may justify booking the revenue prior to shipping. The third level in accounting is *reporting*, the interaction between internal departments or executives and outside auditors. This communication level refers not only to external auditing firms, but also to state or federal regulatory and tax-collecting agencies (sales tax collectors, state income tax authorities, the Internal Revenue Service, and the SEC, for example).

> **Key point:** Accounting operates on three distinct levels: bookkeeping, decision making about the treatment of transactions, and reporting. Keeping these levels in mind helps in understanding how the system works.

On all three of these accounting levels, the existence of documentation and proof is essential. The entire accounting process involves careful and consistent documentation not only of transactions, but also of decisions made during the process. The financial statements are the final step in the methodical accounting process. These statements are the most important parts of the annual report, but they often can be completely understood only by reviewing other sections as well, such as the footnotes.

▲ THE BASICS OF FINANCIAL FORMATTING

The accounting system begins with the recording of transactions within the books of a company. While the routines are largely automated in most big companies, the basic concepts remain unchanged. The steps in the accounting and recording process include the following:

1. *Source documentation.* The starting point of the system is the initial proof—the invoice, statement, receipt, or voucher that proves that a transaction occurred. The original document should provide the amount, date, source (store, company, or person), and business purpose of the transaction. Of course, it would be unwieldy to try and construct a sensible accounting system using the high volume of original documents, so

these are summarized into orderly books and records, beginning with journals.

Key point: Source documents are essential forms of proof; without a source document, a transaction cannot be verified.

2. *Journals.* The second stage of the accounting system is a series of specialized journals. A receipts journal summarizes the company's revenues. So even when the volume of sales is large, the methodical recording of each transaction in the receipts journal enables the accountant to maintain control. If a large amount of revenue is generated on account rather than in cash, a *subsidiary journal* is set up to track each customer's charges and payments. The sum of all customers' activity is added up and recorded in the receipts journal.

A disbursements journal records all money paid out. A large volume of checks would be difficult to record in detail, so the journal enables accountants to summarize a large number of payments by account, and then record a monthly total for each account classification in the general ledger. Subsidiary journals are used for payments as well. For example, if a company employs a petty cash fund for incidental payments that are too small to run through the check-payment system, the sum of activity in the petty cash account is recorded as a single entry in the disbursements journal.

Finally, a general journal is used for recording of all noncash items. These include accruals (recording of revenue that has been earned but for which payment has not yet received in cash, or recording of expenses due this month but not yet paid). Accruals are important if the books are to accurately reflect what happened each month in the company, because actual exchanges of cash often occur in the following month. Accruals show the earned basis of revenue and the accrued basis of costs and expenses. The general journal is also used to set up depreciation and amortization, correct coding errors, or allocate single payments among several categories.

Key point: Journals are devices to collect a volume of material in an orderly manner, classify transactions, and enable accountants to make a smaller number of entries into the ledger at the end of the month.

Terminology of the accounting system. *Depreciation* is a periodic write-off of the cost of capital assets (buildings, equipment, autos and trucks, computers, furniture). Any asset that will last longer than one year should be set up as an asset and depreciated over time. *Amortization* is the recognition of expense over two or more years. For example, suppose a company makes a three-year insurance payment this year. It would be inaccurate to consider the whole payment as an expense this year, so the payment is set up as a prepaid asset; each month, 1/36 of the total is taken out of the asset's value and moved to the Insurance Expense account. After 36 months, the payment is fully amortized.

3. *Ledger entries.* The final book of accounting is the general ledger. This is a summarized version of all the entries in the various journals throughout the month. When the month is over and the books are closed, the journal balances are added up, and the total for each account's total is entered on the appropriate account page in the general ledger. In this way, the number of entries is kept to a minimum, and the general ledger can be more easily kept in balance.

Key point: The general ledger is also called the "book of final entry" because it summarizes a large volume of transactions during the month into a relatively small number of entries. The ledger is balanced before statements are prepared. The sum of all debits has to equal the sum of all credits.

The double-entry mystery. The term "in balance" refers to an important control feature in the accounting system. With double-entry bookkeeping, every entry consists of one or more debits and one or more credits, always of equal value. Debits go on the left side of a journal, and credits go on the right side. They may also be called "plus" and "minus" entries, but that is confusing. They are of equal value. As long as the math is correct throughout all of the journals and in the ledger, the total of all debits should be equal to the total of all credits. If these are not in balance, there is a math error somewhere, and the books cannot be closed until it has been found and corrected.

4. *Financial statements.* The last step in the accounting process is the preparation of financial statements. There are three. The *balance sheet* is a summary of the balances of all asset, liability, and net worth accounts. The sum of assets is always equal to the total of liabilities plus net worth. The *summary of operations* reports revenue, costs, expenses, and profit for a period (quarter or year), and the ending date of the statement always corresponds to the reporting date on the balance sheet. Finally, the *statement of cash flows* summarizes where money came from (sources) and where it was spent (applications). Also called the "sources and applications" statement, the statement of cash flows covers the same time period as the summary of operations.

The complete accounting process is summarized in Figure 2.1.

▲ THE BALANCE SHEET

The first financial statement reports the balances in asset, liability, and shareholders' equity accounts as of a specific date—usually the end of the year or quarter. The sum of all assets is always equal to the combined sum of liabilities plus shareholders' equity accounts.

Many important financial ratios are based on balance sheet accounts (see Chapter 3). For this reason, subtotals of current and long-term assets and liabilities are always reported on the balance sheet. "Current" generally refers to 12 months. A current asset is any asset that is expected to be converted to cash within one year, and a current liability is any debt payable within one year.

FIGURE 2.1

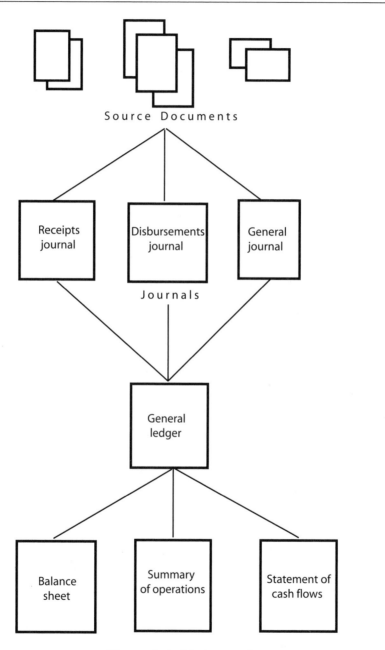

Source Documents

Receipts journal   Disbursements journal   General journal

Journals

General ledger

Balance sheet   Summary of operations   Statement of cash flows

Financial Statements

Key point: The balance sheet reflects balances in asset, liability, and equity accounts as of a specific date. The two other financial statements report activity during a period of time.

The balance sheet has two sections. The first is a listing of all assets; the second is a listing of liabilities and net worth (shareholders' equity). It is subdivided into the following broad classifications:

1. *Current assets.* These are assets that are either in the form of cash or convertible into cash within one year. This category includes cash, accounts receivable (net of a reserve for bad debts), notes receivable, securities, and inventory. Current assets (along with current liabilities) are essential to tracking working capital and judging how well a company manages its cash to fund ongoing operations.

2. *Long-term assets.* These assets, sometimes called "fixed" assets or "capital" assets, are the tangible properties owned by the organization. Within long-term assets are real estate, autos and trucks, equipment and machinery, furniture, computers, and numerous other items. The subtotal is reduced by accumulated depreciation, the aggregate of the annual depreciation expenses claimed. All long-term assets except land are subject to depreciation.

3. *Prepaid assets.* Some expenses are paid in a lump sum but are applicable to more than the current year. For example, a three-year insurance premium is set up as a prepaid asset and amortized over the 36 months.

4. *Deferred assets.* Some payments are made in the current year, but are properly classified in the following year. When the proper period arrives, these deferred assets are removed and reclassified in the proper expense or cost account.

5. *Intangible assets.* Many corporations recognize a value for assets that do not have a physical existence. For example, a company may own noncompete agreements with companies it has purchased assets from, with part of the sale including a promise not to operate a competing activity for a specified period of years. This agreement gives value to the covenant itself, so it is considered an intangible asset. Another major

intangible asset is goodwill, the value of the company's reputation or brand names. In fact, brand name recognition is the result of years of advertising, so goodwill indicates that value. The problem, of course, is establishing a fair dollar value for any intangible asset; for this reason, intangibles are often removed from some important ratios. For example, tangible book value per share excludes this entire classification and divides the tangible net worth by the number of shares outstanding.

6. *Total assets.* The five categories just listed (plus any other specialized subdivisions of assets) are added up, and a total is reported. The total of assets will be the same as the sum of liabilities plus shareholders' equity.

Key point: The distinct classifications of assets are made for good reasons. In order to analyze a company's working capital and overall capital strength, analysts and investors need these breakdowns.

7. *Current liabilities.* These are debts that are due to be paid within the next 12 months. They include accounts payable, payroll taxes payable, interest payable, and the current portion of notes payable (equal to 12 months' payments). The comparison between current assets and current liabilities helps analysts judge a corporation's working capital strength.

8. *Long-term liabilities.* These are debts payable beyond the next 12 months. The category includes long-term notes (excluding the current portion) and bonds payable.

9. *Deferred credits.* It may be that revenue is received in the current year, even though it won't be earned until the next. In this situation, it would be improper to count it as revenue, so it is set up as a deferred credit.

10. *Total liabilities.* The total of all liabilities is shown next, and includes deferred credits as well. The difference between assets and liabilities represents the value of shareholders' equity, as explained later.

Key point: Is the distinction between current and long-term really important? The reason for breaking down liabilities so carefully is found in the tests of working capital and capital strength. Without identifying and distinguishing between current and long-term liabilities, these analyses would be impossible.

11. *Capital stock.* This account shows the value of stock issued and outstanding. For example, if one million shares were issued with a value of $5 per share, then capital stock would be worth $5 million. The value of this account does not change unless additional shares are issued. Capital stock may include common stock (the kind most people buy) and one or more classes of preferred stock. Companies may also buy their own issued shares on the open market, in which case a balance will be shown in an account called Treasury Stock.

12. *Retained earnings.* This is the aggregate of each year's profit or loss. A profit adds to the overall value of shareholders' equity, and a loss reduces that value.

13. *Dividends declared.* When a corporation declares a dividend, that reduces the value of shareholders' equity, and so declared dividends are reported in this section.

14. *Nondeductible expenses.* Some expenses that are not deductible for tax purposes are shown in this section. For example, if a company's drivers receive traffic citations, that is a nondeductible expense.

15. *Total shareholders' equity.* The net total of capital stock, retained earnings, dividends declared, and nondeductible expenses is reported here.

16. *Total liabilities and shareholders' equity.* This is the addition of the two major subtotals, and it will be the same amount as total assets.

How does the balance sheet balance? To nonaccountants, this may seem to be a mystery, but it is really quite logical. Every entry made in the books contains a debit and a credit of equal value. When the books are closed at the end of the period, all profit and loss accounts (revenues, costs, and expenses) are summarized into a single profit number, and that number is added to retained earnings (or, if a loss, subtracted).

As long as all entries have been made correctly, this means that the balance sheet will, in fact, balance. Total assets will have the same value as total liabilities plus shareholders' equity.

The format of the balance sheet and its major divisions is shown in Figure 2.2

In *theory*, all of the information about assets, liabilities, and shareholders' equity that you need is contained in the balance sheet. In reality, as you will discover in Chapter 4, there is far more to the valuation of a company than you find on the balance sheet. First of all, assets are listed at their original value, not their current value. So if a company bought a building 40 years ago and it is now completely depreciated, all that is left on the balance sheet is the original value of the land, with zero value for the improvements. Realistically, that land and building may be worth millions of dollars more today than the balance sheet reports. This works in reverse as well. Many liabilities are not even shown on the balance sheet, such as commitment to long-term leases and the liability for pension and profit-sharing plans. These can be huge numbers, and their exclusion brings up serious questions about whether current accounting rules provide the information that investors need and deserve.

Key point: It is often the case that the most important disclosures are found not on the balance sheet, but in the footnotes. The lack of information on the balance sheet demonstrates how outdated the GAAP rules are.

Another important omission is contingent liabilities. These are obligations that might materialize, or might not. For example, if a lawsuit has been filed against a company, what will the liability be if the company should lose? Consider the case of Merck, which as of 2005 had 6,400 lawsuits pending against it for Vioxx liabilities. This is a very large contingent liability.

▲ THE SUMMARY OF OPERATIONS

The next financial statement—the summary of operations, also called the profit and loss statement or the income statement—reports revenues,

FIGURE 2.2

Company name
Balance Sheet
December 31, 20xx

Assets
    Current Assets
        Cash   xxx

Assets			
Current Assets			
Cash		xxx	
Accounts Receivable	xxx		
Less: Reserve for Bad Debts	(xxx)		
Net		xxx	
Inventory		xxx	
Total Current Assets			xxx
Long-Term Assets:			
Real Estate		xxx	
Equipment and Machinery		xxx	
Autos and Trucks		xxx	
Gross Fixed Assets		xxx	
Less: Accumulated Depreciation		(xxx)	
Net Fixed Assets			xxx
Prepaid Assets			xxx
Deferred Assets			xxx
Intangible Assets			xxx
Total Assets			xxx

Liabilities and Shareholders' Equity			
Current Liabilities			
Accounts Payable		xxx	
Taxes Payable		xxx	
Notes Payable, Current Portion		xxx	
Total Current Liabilities			xxx
Long-Term Liabilities			
Notes Payable		xxx	
Bonds		xxx	
Total Long-Term Liabilities			xxx
Deferred Credits			xxx
Total Liabilities and Deferred Credits			xxx
Shareholders' Equity			
Capital Stock	xxx		
Retained Earnings	xxx		
Dividends Declared	(xxx)		
Nondeductible Expenses	(xxx)		
Total Shareholders' Equity			xxx
Total Liabilities and Shareholders' Equity			xxx

costs, expenses, and profits for a period of time. This period is normally a quarter or a year, and the ending date is always the same as the date used on the balance sheet. For example, if the balance sheet is dated December 31, 2005, the summary of operations would cover a period of time, such as the year, ended December 31, 2005.

The summary of operations contains the following major sections:

1. *Revenues.* Also called sales, this top line of the statement is always the starting point. How much money did the company receive from selling products or services during the indicated period? The revenue line is usually used as the 100 percent value for ratio analysis involving the summary of operations. Gross margin and net profit are expressed as percentages of revenue. In corporations with many different divisions, subsidiaries, or operating units, the total revenue number includes revenues from many different segments. Footnotes should break down revenue into the operating units so that long-term revenue trends can be performed on a per-subsidiary basis.

2. *Returns and allowances.* The second line consists of reductions in revenues. Returns include discounts, cancelled sales, and special provisions granted to customers as part of incentive plans for volume purchases.

3. *Net revenue.* This is the amount remaining when returns and allowances are deducted from gross revenues.

4. *Cost of goods sold.* This section includes many subsections. Costs are items that are directly related to revenues; thus, you would expect to see costs rise or fall along with changes in revenue. Cost items include:

a. *Changes in inventory.* The section starts by listing the inventory at the beginning of the period, and ends by subtracting the ending inventory. The result is to report the net *change* in inventory.

b. *Merchandise or raw materials purchases.* In a manufacturing corporation, raw materials are purchased and then converted into finished goods. In other concerns, such as retail corporations, purchases are the goods bought at wholesale and placed in stores.

c. *Other direct costs.* The company will also report freight (the cost of shipping materials) and direct labor (the cost of manufacturing or processing materials), as well as miscellaneous other costs.

5. *Gross margin.* The net total of direct costs is listed and deducted from net revenues to produce the gross margin. This is the margin earned by the company before deducting expenses.

Key point: A lot of emphasis is placed on revenue trends. However, gross profit trends may be more revealing. As long as the mix of products and services does not change each year, the gross margin as a percentage of revenues should be very consistent.

6. *Expenses.* This may include a number of subclassifications. For example, it is common to divide expenses into "sales and marketing" and "general and administrative" categories. There may be many detailed accounts, so statements of operation often include a single number, with details explained in footnotes or supplementary schedules. Although direct costs are expected to rise and fall with revenues and remain at approximately the same percentage, expenses act differently. You may expect expenses to remain relatively unchanged as long as revenues rise or fall only moderately. However, if revenues grow substantially, you will also see a rise in expenses. This is due to the need for more administrative support staff, facilities rent, equipment depreciation, and the normal day-to-day expenses (office supplies, telephone, utilities, and so on).

Key point: Why do you sometimes see increasing expenses even though revenues and profits are down? When revenues and profits are down but expenses are up, it is an important red flag indicating that management has no control over what is going on in the company.

7. *Operating profit.* This is the difference between gross margin and expenses. It excludes all nonoperating income and expense.

8. *Other income.* Next, income that does not come from normal operations is added. This includes capital gains from selling assets, foreign currency exchange gains, investment profits, interest income, and profits from the sale of a division or unit.

9. *Other expenses.* Nonoperating expenses are deducted next. These include losses from the sale of assets, foreign currency exchange losses, investment losses, interest expense, and losses from the sale of a division or unit.

10. *Pretax profit.* This is operating profit plus other income and less other expenses.

11. *Tax liabilities.* Here the company states what it owes in income taxes.

12. *Net after-tax profit.* The "bottom line" is pretax profit minus liability for income taxes.

One complication in analyzing and comparing statements of operation from one company to another is the inconsistency in how "net profit" is defined. Some analysts may calculate earnings per share or net return using operating profit, whereas others use pretax profit or net after-tax profit. This can be deceptive if you compare two companies, but the numbers being used are not the same.

> **Key point:** For the purpose of judging long-term profitability trends, use operating profit. This makes comparisons between companies valid, and it also ensures that year-to-year changes in nonoperating income and expense do not distort the numbers.

Disagreements may also arise as to whether it is appropriate to use after-tax income to make comparisons in every instance. For example, one corporation may show a huge gain from nonoperating sources this year, while another does not. Thus, the bottom-line comparisons will be inaccurate because they include distortions. A more valid comparison would be to compare operating profit in all cases, so that nonrecurring sources of profit and loss cannot distort the comparison.

The format of the summary of operations is shown in Figure 2.3

▲ THE STATEMENT OF CASH FLOWS

The third statement breaks down the flow of cash into and out of the operation. The concept of *cash flow* is esoteric to many observers. Most

FIGURE 2.3

Company name
Summary of Operations
For the year ending December 31, 20xx

Revenues		xxx
Less: Returns and Allowances		(xxx)
Cost of Goods Sold:		
Inventory, January 1	xxx	
Purchases	xxx	
Direct Labor	xxx	
Freight	xxx	
Total	xxx	
Less: Inventory, December 31		
	(xxx)	
Net Cost of Goods Sold		xxx
Gross Profit		xxx
Expenses:		
Sales and Marketing Expenses	xxx	
General and Administrative Expenses	xxx	
Total Expenses		xxx
Operating Profit		xxx
Other Income		xxx
Other Expenses		(xxx)
Pre-Tax Profit		xxx
Tax Liability		(xxx)
Net After-Tax Profit		xxx

people understand profits and losses, so the summary of operations is easily appreciated. They also understand the concept of valuation, knowing that "shareholders' equity" is the same thing as "net worth," or the actual dollar value of a company. Cash flow is not as easily appreciated.

Cash is the oxygen of any operation. If a company has a chronic shortage of cash, expenses are paid late, and the company may default on loans. The idea of expansion is impossible because that also requires cash. It does not matter how large an amount of accounts receivable is on the books if collections are not current. The statement of cash flows summarizes the all-important cash flow of the operation.

This statement shows—on a cash basis—where the money came from and where it went, ending with the net increase or decrease in cash flow. Sections include the following:

1. *Net profit from operations.* The net profit, or net earnings, is the top line of the statement of cash flows.

2. *Adjustments to net earnings.* Because the net profit includes some noncash items, adjustments have to be made. These include depreciation and amortization. These noncash expenses are added back to net earnings. Because no cash was paid for depreciation and amortization (as it would have been for more typical expense categories), the cash flow is higher.

3. *Cash receipts from other sources.* The company may have received cash proceeds from selling capital assets, from taking out new loans, from issuing new bonds or stock, or from selling off an operating unit.

4. *Changes in current long-term asset and liability accounts.* Cash increases when inventory levels fall, when accounts receivable balances are reduced, when securities are sold off, or when outstanding notes receivable are collected. Cash decreases when inventory levels rise, when accounts receivable balances rise, and when money is loaned out to others. If the level of accounts payable rises, that also increases cash flow; and when it falls, that means that more cash has been paid out, so cash flow falls. The same rule applies to other liability accounts as well.

5. *Dividends paid to shareholders.* Cash flow falls when dividends are paid out to shareholders.

An example of what the statement of cash flows looks like is shown in Figure 2.4.

The three financial statements are linked by date (the date of the balance sheet is the same as the ending date of the other two statements). The three documents are also tied to one another in other ways. The net profit reported in the summary of operations is also used on the statement of cash flows; and when the books are closed, all of the revenue, cost, and expense accounts are turned back to a zero balance, and the net profit is moved over to retained earnings on the balance sheet. These associations are summarized in Figure 2.5.

FIGURE 2.4
___

Company Name
Statement of Cash Flows
For the Year ending December 31, 20xx

Cash flows from operating activities :	
Net earnings	xxx
Adjustments to reconcile net earnings to cash flows:	
Depreciation and amortization	xxx
Changes in assets and liabilities, net of effects from acquisition of businesses:	
Increase in accounts receivable	(xxx)
Decrease in inventories	xxx
Increase in accounts payable and accrued liabilities	xxx
Increase in other current and noncurrent assets	(xxx)
Increase in other current and noncurrent liabilities	xxx
Net cash flows from operating activities	xxx
Additions to property, plant, and equipment	(xxx)
Proceeds from the disposal of assets	xxx
Acquisition of businesses	(xxx)
Purchases of investments	(xxx)
Sales of investments	xxx
Dividends to shareholders	(xxx)
Repurchase of common stock	(xxx)
Proceeds from short-term debt	
Retirement of short-term debt	(xxx)
Proceeds from long-term debt	xxx
Retirement of long-term debt	(xxx)
Net increase (decrease) in cash flow	xxx

FIGURE 2.5

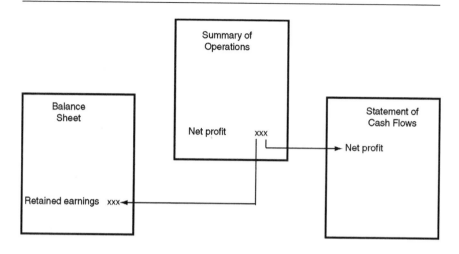

▲ COMPARATIVE STATEMENTS

Any financial information is meaningless unless you are able to compare it with other data. This includes three specific types of comparisons:

1. *Company to company.* A logical and popular method for judging a company's profitability, growth, and financial strength is to make comparisons among companies. For example, you may look at two or three corporations in the same industry (this assumes that the economic and competitive forces are identical). By comparing the results for each company, you can draw obvious conclusions. Levels of sales and sales growth, net return, earnings per share, P/E ratio, and capitalization or working capital tests are all valid methods for comparison.

2. *Results to a universal standard.* The results you see this year can also be compared against a well-understood standard. For example, current ratio is one of the more popular working capital tests, and the standard for "acceptable" is a ratio of 2 to 1 or better (meaning that current assets are at least twice the dollar value of current liabilities). Within a specific industry, a norm or standard for net return may apply as well, and relative comparisons enable you to judge a company's results based on that standard.

3. *Current to historical data.* The annual report usually includes statements on a comparative basis. Thus, you are able to see whether ratios have improved or deteriorated; whether sales and profits have risen or fallen; and whether the company's overall financial condition is stronger or weaker. At the very least, financial statements are normally prepared showing the current full year and the previous full year. In quarterly reports, the quarter and year-to-date are usually compared to the previous year's quarter and year-to-date. An accepted formatting rule is that comparative statements always employ the same number of months. An exception: When a company has been in existence for only a partial year or was merged or acquired during the year, a partial-year report is used.

> **Key point:** Virtually all forms of analysis of the numbers require comparison. Any review of a financial statement by itself is performed in a vacuum.

The normal format for expressing outcomes on the financial statements of major corporations is in millions of dollars. For example, if earnings last year were $426 million, that value would be shown in the annual report as $426 and in the header above the column a notation would be included indicating the abbreviated format: ($000,000) or (in millions).

Another format for comparative data is the multiyear summary. Some corporations include five years' results, and others go out as far as ten years. As with many of the formatting decisions made by companies in their financial reporting, there is no universal standard for how many years to show, or even for what to include. The multiyear comparison usually is not comprehensive, but includes "key" financial data. This usually includes the following:

Balance sheet
    Current assets
    Long-term net assets
    Total assets
    Current liabilities

Long-term liabilities
Shareholders' equity

Summary of Operations
Revenues
Gross profit
Expenses
Operating profit
Net after-tax profit

Other Key Information
Earnings per share
Dividends paid per share
Outstanding shares of common stock
P/E ratio

Because each corporation determines its own "key data" to include, there is no real consistency among corporations. To make consistent comparisons, it is often necessary to go to the more detailed financial statements and footnotes to find everything you need.

Key point: The fact that there is no single standard for how many years of key data to include, or even what to include, makes it quite difficult for anyone to compare corporate financial condition. This is a chronic problem and illustrates how annual reports fail to disclose what you need.

One difficulty in performing any long-term analysis is that results may need to be restated. When an accounting change occurs, for example, it may affect the historical record as well. In this case, corporations restate their historical data so that the latest information is consistent with the record. If this were not done, historical comparisons would be impossible.

Restatements occur as a result of accounting changes (such as valuation methods for inventory), and also when certain other events occur, such as the acquisition of a new subsidiary corporation or sale of an operating unit or subsidiary. In these instances, financial information used in the historical data would be changed to reflect the outcome. For example, if an operating unit is sold, each year's total revenues and earnings would be reduced to report the outcome as if the sold-off unit had not been there for the entire period.

▲ KEEPING IT SIMPLE BUT INFORMATIVE

The typical set of financial statements is not especially complex, when viewed alone. But the information *excluded* from the statements is where you learn what is really going on in the company. This is the reason that footnotes often exceed 100 pages; there is so much to explain about what is not disclosed in the balance sheet, summary of operations, and statement of cash flows that extensive footnotes are necessary. Chapters 5 and 6 examine the complexities of the footnote section and provide guidelines for simplifying and deciphering what the footnotes reveal.

Another problem, perhaps of a more serious nature, is that a lot of information may be excluded from the footnotes, but in fact is material enough that it should be not only included but red-flagged. For example, under GAAP rules, companies are not required to show their pension plan liabilities. This is a staggering flaw in GAAP because pension liabilities can be substantial. In recent years, you have seen news about many corporations, such as United Airlines, filing for bankruptcy because of their pension liabilities. In 2005, the possible bankruptcy of General Motors became a source of speculation once it was discovered that the company's pension liabilities were higher than its entire net worth.

> **Key point:** You cannot rely on what the financial statements disclose without also reviewing the footnotes. The problem, however, is that footnotes are both lengthy and complex. The solution: Identify the *material* potential questions (such as unlisted pension liabilities), and look for the relevant footnotes first.

This raises questions beyond the mere accuracy of the financial statements and the often rosy picture painted in other sections of the annual report. It calls into question both the integrity and the reliability of the accounting industry and the entire system for reporting financial results. Why would you buy stock in a company that was worthless? Shouldn't the facts be put out in plain sight? If, for example, pension liabilities exceed net worth, that means that the stock is worthless as well. It is disappointing for GM stockholders that between 2000 and 2005, the stock's value went from the 55–60 range down to the 20–25 range. But given the disclosure that the company is worthless, the fact that the stock holds any value is amazing. The faith the market shows in the company's ability to somehow regain its basic value is surprising.

The omissions in financial statements reveal the lack of reality in the analysis of companies and in the entire Wall Street culture. Do you buy stocks based on value? And if you do, how do you know whether that value is realistic? Because GAAP allows so many liabilities to be excluded and simply not listed, it is often difficult to identify the real value of a company. If we assume that a stock's value is a reflection of the company's financial strength (real dollars and cents), then the value-based investment decisions made by millions of people are based on misinformation. Chapter 4 details the many substantial items that are left off the financial statements.

For most investors, the unrealistic financial picture painted by traditional financial statements is troubling. However, as the next chapter shows, some basic ratios point the way to identifying viable investment candidates. That chapter explains a few very important ratios and also gives you insights into how corporations can manipulate the numbers to create a favorable outcome. The chapter concludes by presenting five criteria for selecting stocks based on what you find in the annual report, and beyond.

CHAPTER 3

ESSENTIAL RATIOS

ROLLING UP YOUR NUMERICAL SLEEVES

The financial statements are the crucial element in the annual report. In fact, the entire annual report grew from the regulatory requirement that publicly listed companies publish their financial statements both for federal regulators and for stockholders.

The financial statements are published with accompanying schedules and footnotes, and, over time, corporations have expanded the annual report to include many other sections, most of which were designed to promote ownership of shares in the company. The complexity of financial statements—as well as the exclusion of material information—makes it necessary to develop a means for analyzing the numbers to get useful information from the financial disclosures.

Because so much is excluded from the financial statement, this is a very difficult task. In this chapter, you will find a list of valuable ratios and tests that you can use to compare and study companies. Even though important information is excluded from the financial statements, these tests can be used to pick stocks and to decide whether a particular company has the financial strength and profitability that investors should seek. There are three primary areas worthy of analysis: working capital, overall capitalization, and profitability.

▲ REMOVING THE MYSTERY FROM RATIO ANALYSIS

A *ratio* is simply an abbreviated expression of numbers. It reduces two large numbers to a more readily comprehended form. For example, it is easier to understand "3 to 1" than "$416,839.42 to $138,945.33."

Key point: A ratio is nothing more than an abbreviated expression of two larger numbers. It is useful as a shorthand method of analyzing financial facts.

Viewed in isolation, ratios are of only limited value. However, they are the most efficient analytical tool for monitoring long-term trends. In the annual report, the multiyear summary of key financial figures provides the raw material for this analysis, and ratios are easily tracked over time to spot either positive or negative trends. Remember, the ratio is nothing more than an abbreviated representation of dollars-and-cents values.

Ratios are expressed in several different formats, depending on the ratio itself. These formats include:

1. *Factor x to factor y.* The format shown earlier is typical of the "*x* to *y*" format, a reduction of larger numbers to simple ones.

2. *Percentage or numerical value.* Another format is the percentage, used to represent yield or return and other relationships between financial results. A few ratios, such as the price/earnings ratio (P/E) are expressed as a single number, in this case representing the price per share divided by the earnings per share, also called the *multiple.*

3. *Number of occurrences.* Some ratios involve the number of times something takes place, usually on average. For example, inventory *turnover* is a ratio that reveals how many times (on average) inventory is replaced each year. The cost of goods sold is divided by the average value of inventory to determine the number of turns, or

average replacements, as a test of how efficiently a corporation is managing its inventory levels.

These shorthand expressions make long rows and columns of numbers manageable and easier to comprehend. And in reporting by mutual funds, analysis services, and corporations, ratios are effective tools for explaining the significance of a trend. The ratios in such reports use all three of the expression formats. In this chapter, you will find examples of each of the expression formats. As a general rule, each commonly used ratio tends to appear in the same format whenever it is given.

A second tool that helps to make analysis manageable is averaging. A simple average is well known to most people. A field of values or results is added together, and then the total is divided by the number of values. For example, if you want to find the average of 632, 415, and 510, you add the three values together and then divide by 3:

$$632 + 415 + 510 = 1,557$$
$$1,557 \div 3 = 519$$

Analysis of stock ratios and stock pricing trends often employs a moving average. In its basic form, a moving average represents a series of results over time. Each time the average is calculated, the oldest value is dropped and the latest is added. Most online stock charting services, for example, show a history of price movements along with a 200-day moving average. When recent prices have been volatile, that volatility can make it difficult to see the longer-term price trend. A moving average, especially one involving a large number of fields, evens out the volatility.

The same is true in analysis of financial results. In short-term studies, elements such as revenues and earnings tend to be chaotic and volatile, making it difficult to spot a broader trend. But when a moving average is used, it makes the analysis more sensible. Just as the ratio reduces complex numbers to a simple form, the moving average reduces a range of results and outcomes to a recognizable trend and direction.

There are several variations on moving averages that are used by statisticians and market analysts. A complex variation of the moving average is called the exponential moving average (EMA). This gives greater weight, or importance, to the most recent data. A weighted moving average may be calculated by hand as well. For example, for a field of three values, you may count the most recent value twice and divide the total by 4:

$$632 + 415 + 510 + 510 = 2,067$$
$$2,067 \div 4 = 516.75$$

When these various methods of averaging are applied to a larger field of entries, the process can become complex. It can be simplified by using spreadsheet programs like Excel, or by relying on the many online services that provide information, including moving averages. Once you determine the formula, programming the calculation into a spreadsheet program is easy. Referring to the formula given here for a weighted moving average, an Excel spreadsheet formula employing a single column of numbers would be:

ROW	COLUMN A
1	VALUE 1
2	VALUE 2
3	VALUE 3
4	FORMULA: =SUM(1A:3A) (TOTAL OF ALL VALUES)
5	FORMULA: =SUM(4A+3A) (TOTAL PLUS WEIGHTED VALUE)
6	FORMULA: =SUM(5A/4) (WEIGHTED AVERAGE)

With this simple formula, you simply need to enter the three values in the first three rows, and the program automatically recalculates the weighted moving average.

Key point: The moving average is valuable for giving a long-term view of a trend, especially when period-to-period changes tend to be erratic.

In any form of analysis, you will want to maintain a realistic outcome. This is as true for the financial statements in the annual report as for anywhere else. Therefore, atypical information should be excluded from any trend analysis. For example, consider the following example of annual revenues:

YEAR	REVENUES
1	$416,311
2	421,007
3	420,515
4	703,994
5	422,613
6	426,089
7	427,440

Clearly, the range of revenue levels extends from $416,311 to $427,440, and the results in the fourth year are extraordinarily out of line with this range. Further examination may reveal the reasons for this, which could include nonrecurring sales or some type of correction of previous errors. Whatever the reason, the fourth year is about $280,000 higher than the typical level. To calculate what is likely to happen in year 8 and into the future, it would be inaccurate to include the fourth year's total. The *spike* of about $280,000 should be removed from the study to ensure that estimates of future revenue levels are not distorted. A moving average would level out some of the problem, but you can make the numbers more reliable by (1) identifying the cause of the spike and, (2) upon determining that it was a one-time aberration, removing it from the analysis.

This rule applies to all types of trend analysis. The financial statements you find in the annual report are flawed because they represent today's valuation or the latest year's results. They are not designed to interpret those results, only to provide them. Ratios and adjusted averaging techniques are important tools for interpreting the numbers and, more to the point, for making that interpretation as reliable as possible.

▲ THE FINITE NUMBER OF RATIOS YOU NEED TO KNOW

There is a tendency to think that once you get involved in analyzing financial statements, footnotes, and other money-oriented parts of the annual report, you need to perform a comprehensive and detailed review. This is not so; you can gain a lot of valuable information with only a handful of ratios.

> **Key point:** You do not need to master dozens of ratios. A handful of revealing indicators is all you need to gain an overview of financial results.

Becoming an expert in accounting takes many years of experience. For this reason, investors can be intimidated by the 100-plus pages of footnotes and the unintelligible explanations. While knowing how to interpret this information is a valuable skill, you can get by with only the following ratios:

1. Working capital.
The *current ratio* compares current assets and liabilities.
The *quick assets ratio* is similar to the current ratio, but without inventory.
Inventory turnover compares inventory and direct costs.

2. Capitalization.
The *debt ratio* shows the sources from which operations are funded.

3. Profitability.
Gross margin compares gross profit to revenues.
Expense level is a study of expenses as a percentage of revenues.
Net return compares earnings to revenues.

In addition to the ratios in these three classifications, you can learn a lot by checking dividend yield and the consistency of dividends paid over time, the well-known P/E ratio, and some technical indicators, such as the 52-week price range and a review of the trading range.

▲ WORKING CAPITAL RATIOS

Working capital refers to the amount of cash available. This *liquidity* factor is crucial to the running of a business operation. Cash is needed to pay ongoing liabilities, to make payroll, to order merchandise, and, in the longer term, to fund expansion.

If a company's cash flow is weak, that inhibits its ability to remain competitive and to produce the goods or services that its customers require. The most popular test of working capital is the *current ratio*, which examines and compares current assets and current liabilities. "Current" means assets that either are in the form of cash or are convertible to cash within 12 months; current liabilities are those that are due and payable within 12 months. To calculate the current ratio, divide current liabilities by current assets, expressing the answer in the x to y format:

$$\frac{\text{CURRENT ASSETS}}{\text{CURRENT LIABILITIES}} = X \text{ TO } Y$$

A general standard for the current ratio is 2 to 1. A company is considered to be in good shape if its current ratio is 2 to 1 or better, and, with some exceptions, when the current ratio is less than 2 to 1, this is considered negative. This standard is not universal, however. Very large corporations—those with assets in the billions, for example—can claim to have a healthy working capital position even when the current ratio is lower than 2 to 1. The real danger occurs when the ratio becomes less than 1. For example, if the current ratio were 1 to 2, meaning that there were twice as many current liabilities as current assets, that would be a danger signal.

> **Key point:** Working capital is an indicator of how well a company manages its money, plans for timely payment of bills, and plans for long-term growth. Cash flow is the essential oxygen that keeps a company alive.

All ratios can be affected by the timing of payments, and the current ratio is no exception. For example, consider what happens when the following situation exists near the end of the year:

CURRENT ASSETS	$15,611,004
CURRENT LIABILITIES	$ 9,409,441
CURRENT RATIO	1.7 TO 1

Now consider how the ratio would change if the company paid off $3 million in current liabilities before closing out the year:

CURRENT ASSETS	$12,611,004
CURRENT LIABILITIES	$ 6,409,441
CURRENT RATIO	2.0 TO 1

One of the often overlooked realities of ratio analysis is that the timing of transactions by the corporation affects the outcome. This is troubling because you have to wonder: Would the company pay off those current liabilities just before the end of the year if the current ratio were not an important test of working capital? In other words, to what extent do companies adjust the timing of their transactions with these ratios in mind?

Even the decision on exactly when to close the books will affect ratios. By closing two days earlier than usual, or one day later, the values of many ratios can be affected, especially if the fiscal year ends in a high-volume month. For example, in a large retail establishment, high-volume months like November and December often account for virtually all of the year's profits. So the decision on when to close the books will have a significant effect on the values of all ratios.

Closing the books is an accounting term referring to the cutting off of transactions for a fiscal period (a month or quarter or year). The accounting department picks a day to close the books, and all transactions to be included in the current period end on that day. Any transactions taking place *after* the books are closed go into the next accounting period. In a high-volume month, the decision to close the books on the 26th or 27th of the month excludes all revenue, costs, and expenses generated after those dates; and if the books for December are not closed until January 2, a similar—and potentially significant—change in what gets reported in December's results may occur.

The current ratio is an important test of working capital, but it is not the final answer by any means. Investors who have never worked in a corporation's accounting department tend to view the accounting process in pure terms. There is one "correct" representation of a month or a year, and the totals of assets and liabilities (as well as the totals of revenue, costs, expenses, and profits) are accepted as realistic. In practice, these outcomes can be manipulated without much effort.

Even if you accept the validity of a company's timing for purposes of studying the current ratio, this ratio is not the only test of working capital. In corporations with significant levels of inventory, the current ratio is often lower than 2 to 1, out of necessity because inventories are offset by higher accounts payable. For example, a manufacturing concern may need to invest in raw materials and also report large dollar values for work in process and finished goods. Because seasonal volume varies widely, it is possible that year-end inventory levels will be quite high. Does this mean that a low current ratio indicates a problem with working capital?

For example, a particular company manufactures goods throughout the year and closes its books in December. At that time, sales volume is relatively low, but inventory levels and accounts payable balances tend to be higher than they are during the warmer months. The year-end numbers show:

CURRENT ASSETS:	
INVENTORY	$ 6,405,900
ALL OTHER CURRENT ASSETS	19,806,211
TOTAL	$26,212,111
CURRENT LIABILITIES	$18,903,554
CURRENT RATIO	1.4 TO 1

About one-fourth of all current assets are in inventory, so this account has a lot of influence on the current ratio. In these circumstances, a second working capital ratio is used. It is called the *quick assets ratio* or the *quick ratio* or *acid test ratio*. This is the current ratio, excluding inventory. The general standard defining a "good" level for the quick assets ratio is 1 to 1. So if the quick assets are equal to or higher than the total current liabilities, that is acceptable.

For example, given the values in the previous example, the quick assets ratio is:

CURRENT ASSETS EXCLUDING INVENTORY	$19,806,211
CURRENT LIABILITIES	$18,903,554
QUICK ASSETS RATIO	1.0 TO 1

Inventory is a significant factor in the evaluation of working capital, whether you are using the current ratio or the quick assets ratio. However, inventory is probably the least liquid of all the current assets, so excluding it from the working capital test often sheds more light on the real working capital situation than the current ratio does.

> **Key point:** While current assets are defined as assets that are in the form of cash or are convertible to cash within 12 months, some current assets are more liquid than others. Inventory is the least liquid of current assets.

A third test, which evaluates the company's efficiency in handling and maintaining inventory levels, is *inventory turnover*. This is a study of the number of "turns" that take place per year, or the number of times that inventory is used up and replaced.

> **Turnover realities:** Inventory turnover is an *average* based on average inventory levels. In practice, inventory is not depleted and then replaced. However, by dividing inventory by a company's direct costs, you produce an estimate of the company's efficiency in managing inventory levels. If a company is carrying slow-moving stock, for example, the number of turns will decline.

The formula for inventory turnover involves dividing the cost of goods sold by the average inventory level:

$$\frac{\text{DIRECT COSTS}}{\text{AVERAGE INVENTORY}} = \text{TURNS}$$

The result is provided as a simple number (without a percent sign or other indicator). For example, if direct costs for the year were $213.6 million and average inventory was $47.3 million, turnover would be:

$$\frac{213.6}{47.3} = 4.5 \text{ TURNS}$$

There is no single standard for an "acceptable" number of turns. However, by studying a corporation's inventory turnover over time, you can spot trends. It is particularly interesting to observe how turnover changes as revenue increases. In the best of all worlds, turnover would remain steady even when revenues grow substantially. However, there is a tendency for turnover to slow down with greater volume.

Finding *average* inventory in the annual report can be a potential problem. You may need to look at the company's quarterly financial statements in order to determine whether year-end inventory is representative for the entire year. In some corporations, inventory levels remain fairly stable, so "average" can simply require taking the beginning and ending balances and using the average of the two. But other companies experience wide seasonal swings in inventory levels, and the real average could be more complex. A quarter-end inventory level could be used to get a more realistic average, for example. The four quarter-end inventory levels are added together and divided by 4 to find a more representative average.

The three working capital ratios are summarized in Figure 3.1.

▲ CAPITALIZATION

One area that is often overlooked in financial statement analysis is the nature of the company's *capitalization.* Total capitalization—the source

FIGURE 3.1

Current Ratio	Quick Assets Ratio	Inventory Turnover
$\dfrac{CA}{CL} = x \text{ to } y$	$\dfrac{CA - I}{CL} = x \text{ to } y$	$\dfrac{DC}{AI} = n$

CA = current assets
CL = current liabilities
I = inventory
DC = direct costs
AI = average inventory

of a corporation's total capital—comes from two primary sources: capital stock and long-term debt.

The importance of capitalization is easily ignored when too much emphasis is placed on maintaining a healthy level of working capital. As a consequence, the current ratio has become a prominent and important test. But it can easily mislead you if you are not also aware of how capitalization trends work.

> **Key point:** Capitalization is simply the funding of a company. It comes from two general sources. *Equity* is provided by investors, who expect dividends and stock price appreciation. *Debt* comes from lenders, who expect periodic interest payments and repayment of the amount loaned.

Capital stock—equity capitalization—may appreciate in value over time and yield returns to shareholders in two ways: price appreciation from higher market value, which is widely understood, and dividend yield. But many investors are not fully aware of how the long-term value of the stock and the continuation of dividends are threatened when the other type of capitalization—debt capitalization—increases over time. This debt, in the form of long-term notes and bonds issued by the corporation, can have a negative effect on long-term growth in several ways. First, the higher the amount of debt is, the higher the future debt service, or repayment obligation. Second, the higher the amount of debt is, the greater the interest expense will be. There is a natural competition for operating profit dollars between dividends (to stockholders) and interest (to note- and bondholders).

The ratio that everyone needs to understand is called the *long-term debt to equity* ratio. This calculation, expressed as a percentage, is calculated by adding together the long-term debt and total shareholders' equity and dividing long-term debt by that total:

$$\frac{\text{LONG-TERM DEBT}}{\text{LONG-TERM DEBT} + \text{STOCKHOLDERS' EQUITY}} = \frac{\text{LONG-TERM DEBT}}{\text{TO EQUITY RATIO}}$$

In many respects, this ratio is more important than the current ratio, especially when you are looking at long-term growth prospects. And unless you look at both ratios together, you can get a false picture of what is going on in the corporation. For example, during a period when the company is losing money every year, several trends develop. These include reduced sales and earnings and declining working capital. Many analysts keep an eye on the current ratio to ensure that even when losses occur, the company's overall health remains strong.

Now consider the problem if a company begins accumulating long-term debt and keeps the proceeds in cash. The current ratio can be maintained at what appears to be a healthy level, but long-term debt continues to grow. The information is all there in the annual report, but the negative trend is easily missed. Consider the case of Motorola in the four years from 1999 to 2002. In this period, the company's sales and earnings were declining, but the current ratio *improved*. How is this possible?

According to the Motorola annual report (and with detailed summaries provided by the Standard & Poor's Stock Report for Motorola), the results shown in Table 3.1 applied for these years.

Taking this information from the annual report, the first thing you notice is the disappointing trend in sales and earnings. Sales fell each year, and for the last two years the company reported net losses. At the same time, the current ratio improved. How is this possible? By definition, you would expect to see a weakening current ratio following a $5.8 billion loss. The answer is found in the growing debt ratio. During the same period, the debt ratio increased from 15.3 percent to 40.6 percent. This means that debt was 15.3 percent of total capitalization at he end of 1999, but 40.6 percent of the total at the end of 2002. This explains how the current ratio was not only maintained, but improved.

TABLE 3.1   ANNUAL RESULTS, MOTOROLA.

	Results (in millions of dollars) *			
	2002	2001	2000	1999
Net Sales	$27,279	$30,486	$38,136	$33,693
Operating Earnings	(1,813)	(5,803)	895	230
	Ratios *			
Current Ratio	1.7 to 1	1.8 to 1	1.2 to 1	1.3 to 1
Debt ratio	40.6%	39.3%	19.2%	15.3%

* Sources: *www.motorola.com* annual report; and Standard & Poor's Stock Report for Motorola, Inc.

> **Key point:** Outcomes are not always what they seem. It is possible to conclude that working capital is healthy without realizing that the ratio has been created by growth in long-term debt. Invariably, apparent trends have to be confirmed by also checking other, related trends.

The key here was in the sales and earnings trends, which were clearly moving in a negative direction. In that situation, it is not possible to maintain the current ratio unless long-term debt is increased. In this case, the current ratio was maintained by increasing the dollar value of cash during the four years. The proceeds from the new long-term debt were kept in the form of cash, so the result was maintenance of the current ratio.

From the isolated analysis of cash flow, involving a comparison between current assets and current liabilities, it appeared that all was well. However, when you further consider the ramifications over the long term, it becomes clear that the current ratio by itself is not enough. The significant shift toward higher debt capitalization means that future net earnings will be used to pay a growing burden of interest. Assuming that Motorola's long-term prospects are favorable, it will be difficult for the company to maintain or improve dividend payments, because net earnings will have to be spent on interest expense.

This type of analysis can be performed using information found in the annual report, supplemented with additional material from analytical services, such as Standard & Poor's. In fact, Motorola's annual report disclosures do not provide enough detail to make this kind of analysis. The information from the S&P Stock Report is provided as a free feature on the Charles Schwab web site at https://investing.schwab.com and is available to subscribers. Many other trading web sites offer similar supplementary services to subscribers.

▲ PROFITABILITY

Another area where ratio analysis is revealing concerns the question of profitability. Long-term trends are crucial for determining whether or not a company will be able to continue growing, and, in fact, whether growth has occurred at all. Every company hopes to earn increasing revenues and profits each year, but that is not always the case.

Whether sales levels grow, remain the same, or decline, three specific ratios can reveal the health of the operation: gross margin, expense level, and net return. At the very least, if you expect to invest money in a corporation, you need to ensure that its long-term growth prospects are strong. The most reliable indicator of growth potential is a demonstrable ability to create and maintain profitability.

For some analysts, tracking revenue over time is a priority. Revenues should rise each year, according to this school of thought; and if revenues flatten out or decline, that is thought of as a negative indicator. This belief may be misguided for several reasons:

1. *Cyclical change has much to do with revenue levels.* Most businesses have to operate within business cycles that may last from a few months to many years. These cycles often affect revenue growth trends. It may be unrealistic to expect revenues to continue growing at the same rate indefinitely.

2. *Nothing continues growing at the same pace.* Statistically, it is impossible to sustain the same *rate* of growth every year. For example, 10 percent growth on $1 million is $100,000. So if next year's revenues are $1.1 million, is it realistic to expect sales in the third year to grow by another 10 percent, or $110,000? Growth trends will tend to flatten out over time when studied on a percentage basis.

3. *Competitive forces limit potential growth, because markets are finite.* Every market is defined by its limitations. There are going to be only so many consumers within one industry, and several companies will be competing for those consumers. Because of this, no industry will continue growing forever, and no one company can have an ever-larger market share unless it eliminates its competitors.

4. *Top-line (revenue) growth is nowhere near as important as earnings.* Ultimately, revenue growth is worthless if, at the same time, profits are shrinking. No matter what level of revenue the com-

pany generates, its profitability is far more important and affects long-term growth and the stock price more than revenue growth alone does.

As a starting point in judging how well a corporation manages its operations, check the *gross margin*. The gross margin, defined as profit after deducting direct costs but before deducting expenses, should be consistent over time. Look at several years' results to ensure that this is the case. If the gross margin diminishes as revenues increase, that is a sign of poor internal controls. Assuming that there is no change in the mix of products and services, gross margin is an excellent starting point in determining whether the company is in control of its growth.

Gross margin may change over time. When gross margin changes from one year to the next, this may indicate internal control problems, but does not always do so. If the company has merged with or acquired another company, the new mix of revenues may cause a change in gross margin; the same thing can happen when a company sells one of its operating units. As a first step, when you see a change in gross margin, go to the footnotes and look for two specific notes: "Mergers, acquisitions, and partnerships" explains changes in corporate segments, and "segment information" breaks down revenues and direct costs by major segments or lines of business.

To calculate gross margin, divide gross profit by revenues. On the statement of operations, most ratios are reflected as a percentage of revenues, and this is no exception. The gross profit is what remains after direct costs are deducted from revenues:

$$\frac{\text{GROSS PROFIT}}{\text{REVENUES}} = \text{GROSS MARGIN}$$

Gross margin becomes meaningful only if and when an established level changes. For example, review the following summary:

Year	Revenues	Direct Costs	Gross Profit	Gross Margin
1	$416,311	$160,664	$255,647	61.4%
2	424,562	164,307	260,255	61.3
3	430,995	166,801	264,194	61.3
4	431,582	180,301	251,281	58.2
5	437,004	191,446	245,558	56.2

An established level of about 61 percent gross margin begins to slip in the fourth and fifth years, which is a significant, apparently negative trend. However, before concluding that the trend is negative, check the changes in segment revenues and costs to see whether the mix of business changed in the fourth and fifth years. The trend may indicate a lack of control, or it may reflect a change in the makeup of the segments.

Key point: Gross margin should remain consistent regardless of sales volume. Assuming that management does its job properly, you should not see changes in gross margin from one year to the next unless the business mix changes.

A second test of profitability involves a review of expenses as a percentage of sales. This is calculated by dividing expenses by total revenues:

$$\frac{\text{EXPENSES}}{\text{REVENUES}} = \text{EXPENSE LEVEL}$$

It is discouraging to see growth in expenses exceed the growth in the top line, and it is even more disturbing when revenues fall but expenses rise. Consider this example:

Year	Revenues	Expenses	Expense Level
1	$704,378	$210,290	29.9%
2	698,088	215,439	30.9
3	691,473	216,043	31.2
4	687,381	221,413	32.2
5	674,018	226,510	33.6

In this situation, revenues declined each year, but expenses rose—not only the amount of expenses, but the percentage as well. This is a very troubling situation. Most analysts would agree that when revenues fall or remain the same, expenses should follow suit. In fact, when revenues rise, the ideal situation is for expenses to remain at approximately the same percentage, or even to fall as a percentage of sales.

The last profitability test is also among the best-known ratios, *net return*. This is the operating profit expressed as a percentage of revenues:

$$\frac{\text{NET OPERATING PROFIT}}{\text{REVENUES}} = \text{NET RETURN}$$

Why use operating profit rather than net earnings after other income and expense? The operating earnings reflect the outcome based on the primary, or core, activity of the company and exclude nonoperating profit or loss, such as capital gains, currency exchanges, or the profit from selling an operating unit. These are nonrecurring sources of earnings, and it is inaccurate to include them in a year-to-year study of net earnings.

The primary profitability ratios are summarized in Figure 3.2.

▲ SHARE PRICE RATIOS AND DIVIDEND YIELD

Two additional ratios have to be included in any analysis of financial information found in the annual report: earnings per share (EPS) and

FIGURE 3.2

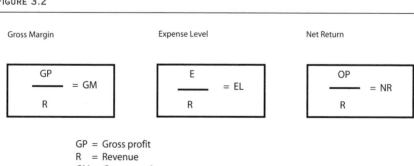

Gross Margin   Expense Level   Net Return

$$\frac{GP}{R} = GM \qquad \frac{E}{R} = EL \qquad \frac{OP}{R} = NR$$

GP = Gross profit
R = Revenue
GM = Gross margin
E = Expenses
EL = Expense level
OP = Operating profit
NR = Net return

dividend yield. As with all ratios, it is important to study the trend in these ratios over time. For example, you would expect that a corporation that was experiencing steady growth would also report ever-higher earnings per share. And dividend yield should remain consistent or improve slightly each year.

> **Key point:** Share price and dividend yield are momentary indicators based on ever-changing market conditions. They may provide some insight, but they should not be given too much importance in a financial review, as they are not really financial at all.

Earnings per share is derived by a process of division. Earnings have to be defined carefully, however. As with previous ratios, which number do you use? The net operating profit (before other income and expense and before taxes) is the most reliable. The nonoperational and nonrecurring adjustments to operating profit cannot be accurately counted as part of the ongoing core profitability of the company; so EPS should be determined using operating profit. The number of shares may also need adjustment. If the company issued additional shares during the year, you need to use an average to calculate EPS. If shares were issued relatively early or late in the year, you may also need to weight the average to approximate a true yearlong average of shares outstanding (in the hands of investors).

Once you have identified the proper total earnings and number of shares, EPS is calculated as follows:

$$\frac{\text{NET OPERATING PROFIT}}{\text{TOTAL SHARES OUTSTANDING}} = \text{EPS}$$

EPS is expressed in dollars and cents. For example, if net operating profit for the year was $612,610,005 and the total number of shares outstanding was 300,000,000, EPS is calculated as:

$$612,610,005 \div 300,000,000 = \$2.04$$

Dividend yield is an oddity because it compares the currently paid dividends per share to the price of the stock. This is odd because dividends are considered a fundamental attribute of the company, but share price is technical, or market-related. Investors include dividend yield as one of many factors in comparing stocks and in picking stocks to include in their portfolio.

The yield is calculated by dividing the dividends paid each year by the current market price of the stock:

$$\frac{\text{DIVIDENDS PAID}}{\text{SHARE PRICE}} = \text{DIVIDEND YIELD}$$

For example, suppose a company pays 15 cents per share each quarter, which is an annual dividend of 60 cents per share. The current price per share is 22.00. Dividend yield is computed as:

$$0.60 \div 22.00 = 2.7\%$$

In tracking dividend yield at the end of the year as summarized in the annual report, you face two problems:

1. The year-end price of the stock might not reflect the *typical* price of the stock before and after the precise date of the statement. For example, suppose that a stock typically trades between $30 and $35 per share. At December 31, the price dips to $22.00 for three days and then returns to its more typical trading pattern. In this case, the reported year-end dividend yield is misleading.

2. The yield changes each time the stock price changes. The lower the price, the higher the dividend yield. For example, a company paying 60 cents per year would show the following dividend yield at various stock prices:

STOCK PRICE	DIVIDEND YIELD
$34	1.8%
30	2.0
26	2.3
22	2.7

With a fixed dividend per share and a changing price, the actual dividend yield can be deceiving. Over a long period of time, investors expect dividends to keep pace with an increasing stock price; but an unchanging dividend payment can look better each year when the stock's price ebbs lower, so the long-term trend in dividend yield can be deceiving.

> **Key point:** Dividend yield is meaningful only in relation to the price you pay for stock. After that, changes in the yield don't affect you. Even though yield is reported in the financial pages every day, it counts only on the day you buy the stock.

The dividend yield at the price they pay for stock is useful to investors. The yield at that price is, in fact, the yield they continue to earn no matter how long they hold the stock, as long as the dividend doesn't change, because it is based on the actual amount paid for stock. If you are reviewing an annual report to search for multiyear trends, you need to look at the dividend paid rather than the yield. If the company has increased its dividends per share each year, that is an important indicator, regardless of the year-to-year dividend yield.

▲ THE P/E RATIO

The annual report summarizes the key financial data, which includes revenues, profits, assets, and liabilities—and the P/E ratio, which is one of the most popular measurements of stock. A lot of attention is paid to P/E, which is a summary of the price per share as a *multiple* of earnings. P/E is computed by dividing the price per share by EPS, and the ratio is shown as a numerical value:

$$\frac{\text{SHARE PRICE}}{\text{EPS}} = \text{P/E}$$

So when the EPS is $2.04 and the current price per share is $22.00, the P/E is:

$$\frac{\$22.00}{\$2.04} = 10.8$$

The current price is equal to 10.8 times current (or latest) earnings. The higher the P/E multiple is, the greater the market's belief in the company's future earnings potential. Of course, higher-P/E stocks also tend to be higher risk.

Like dividend yield, P/E changes each time the stock price moves. There are several problems with relying on the year-end P/E that you find in the annual report. These include:

1. *Disparity between the two values.* The price is always the current price of the stock, but the earnings may be several months out of date. For example, in the middle of the first quarter, the latest earnings are for the previous year. If the company is in the middle of an annual cycle, this may distort the P/E and make it unreliable.

2. *Potential inaccuracy in share price.* The share price reported at the end of the year and used in the annual report might not be typical for the company's trading range. This will distort the reported P/E at year-end, making year-to-year tracking difficult and of questionable value.

3. *Inflated earnings included in the equation.* If the company's reported profits include nonrecurring income or leave out some expenses, the P/E and other ratios are going to be inaccurate. For this reason, it makes more sense to use a computed core earnings value in calculating the P/E.

Key point: The P/E ratio can be very unreliable unless it uses current information for both sides of the equation. Thus, a year-end P/E found in the annual report is not necessarily a fair reflection of historical trends.

The solution to these problems is to use a comparative P/E based on average share price rather than on the price at the end of the year. The annual comparisons between P/Es are not especially valuable, because they are historical and may not reflect what is going on today. P/E is a useful indicator for anyone comparing stocks at the time an investment decision is being made. But even though annual report analysts place great importance on the year-to-year P/E, it is potentially misleading.

▲ TECHNICAL INDICATORS THAT YOU NEED

The summary of key financial results found in the annual report can confuse investors by including both financial and nonfinancial information. The financial, also called *fundamental*, indicators include revenues, earnings, capitalization, and dividends declared and paid. The nonfinancial, also called *technical*, indicators include high and low stock prices during the year and the year-end stock price per share. These are important forms of information, but there are distinct differences as well. As demonstrated in the previous section, using snapshot information for nonfinancial indicators can distort the real picture, so these indicators have to be reviewed with their limitations in mind. Even the P/E ratio is a hybrid, consisting of both technical (price) and fundamental (earnings per share) information.

There are a few technical indicators that are useful in an overall analysis of the annual report. These include the 52-week high and low prices of the stock and the year's trading range. Both of these technical indicators provide useful information about the market risk of the stock.

> **Key point:** Most investors claim to follow either fundamental or technical indicators. But in reality, both can provide insights concerning valuation, growth potential, and market risk.

The 52-week high/low range is valuable, but it should be accompanied by a review of the year's trading chart as well. For example, consider the case in which a stock has a reported 52-week trading range of 21/42. This means that the stock traded between $21 per share and $42 per share. Investors like to look at the 52-week high/low range and then draw conclusions about the stock's current price. But this can be misleading. For example, the following possibilities may be discovered when you also look at a price chart:

1. *The trading range might include a nonrecurring spike.* In some instances, a *spike*—an unusual change in price—might have occurred. As long as it was isolated and the price range returned to a previously established trading range, the spike should be removed from the analysis. For example, a 52-week high/low shows that trading occurred between $21 and $42 per share. But the majority of the trading occurred between $21 and $26, and a one-time spike to $42 occurred because of a takeover rumor that proved to be untrue. In this situation, the 52-week high/low is not accurate.

2. *The price might be showing an upward trend.* The high/low summary does not tell you about the actual price trend. If the stock has been moving steadily upward, that is important information, so a review of the price should include looking at the 52-week chart as well.

3. *The price might be showing a downward trend.* The same rule can apply when prices are trending downward. A 52-week high/low is only a summary of the entire range; it does not reveal the longer-term direction of price movement.

4. *Volatility in price might make it impossible to spot a trend.* When prices change unpredictably in either direction, it is impossible to spot a trend. Price volatility makes a stock higher risk, and this is an important element. For example, a 21/42 high/low could reflect a steadily rising or falling price trend, or it could reflect an erratic series of gyrations in the price, with no discernible price direction.

The 52-week high/low range is a useful indicator, but it is only a starting point. The annual report may include this test of volatility, but it is unlikely that the significance of the trading range will be explained. As a passive document, the annual report provides raw material but usually does not tell you what that material means.

Key point: The 52-week high/low can mislead you and cause you to reach an inaccurate conclusion. You should also review a 52-week price chart to spot the trend within that trading range.

The 52-week high/low is a summary of a full year's price range, but that is not always the same as the trading range. What is the usual gap between a stock's high and low price? By judging the volatility in a stock's price, defined by the number of points in the normal range, you can draw conclusions about a stock's market risk. So a high/low between $21 and $42 per share could result from a very wide trading range, meaning that the stock is very volatile. Or the trading range could be quite narrow, with the overall price trending upward or downward during the year.

Therefore, the high/low usually included in the annual report is not enough to allow you to draw conclusions about the stock's market risk. The price chart also has to be reviewed so that you can see, within the context of the 52 weeks, how the trading range has emerged. This makes it easier to estimate future volatility and potential price movement.

The entire annual report is based on financial results, interpreted through comparisons between years and calculated ratios. The report then includes management's explanations, found in footnotes; management's discussion of the financial statements; and the public relations section explaining what the company provides in its markets. But the application of ratios requires a view of the long-term trend and, quite often, applying interpretive conclusions that management does not provide in its financial raw material. You may conclude that what management provides in the annual report is passive, and that you need to interpret it for yourself. But perhaps more alarming is what you do *not* find on the financial statements. Chapter 4 explains what is left off the financial statements and how those exclusions often affect all of the conclusions you draw.

CHAPTER 4

WHAT STATEMENTS DO NOT REVEAL

DIRTY LITTLE ACCOUNTING SECRETS

One of the serious flaws in the way financial reporting takes place is the lack of complete information in the financial statements. The widespread belief that financial statements are complete is simply wrong. So many significant and material items are excluded from the statements that they cannot be relied upon for establishing valuations of companies.

The problem is best appreciated by comparison. If you were to make an offer on a piece of real estate, the closing process would include a title search. Any liens against the property would be paid off from the proceeds of the sale, and you would acquire clean title to the property. While this makes perfect sense, the same process does not apply when you buy shares of stock.

> **Key point:** In real estate, the rules require that you know the true value of property that you buy. But in the stock market, this is not the case.

If you discovered after closing that your new real estate purchase was worthless because several liens had not been disclosed during the closing, you would be upset. However, when you buy shares of stock, you rely on the valuation reported in the financial statements to establish that the company has equity and earnings potential. This is not always the case. In fact, many companies do not include all of their liabilities on their balance sheet, and the accounting rules say that this is perfectly all right.

▲ OFF-BALANCE-SHEET LIABILITIES

Many liabilities do not show up on the balance sheet even though they are very real. You need to study the footnotes in detail to find out about these often substantial debts. This means that the net worth of the company may be far lower than you have been led to believe. Some examples:

1. *Pension liabilities.* Under the accounting rules, companies are not required to report their liabilities to employees who will retire in the future. Because of pension liabilities, many of the largest corporations have no net worth. These include companies like United Airlines, which was bankrupted by pension debts in 2005, and General Motors, which owes more in pension payments than its entire net worth.

2. *Off-balance-sheet obligations.* The infamous complexity of Enron's multitude of off-balance-sheet subsidiaries, partnerships, and proposed mergers is an extreme example. But in fact, many corporations have liabilities that are not included on the balance sheet. Long-term lease obligations are very real liabilities, but accounting rules do not require some of them to be shown on the books. They are disclosed in footnotes only. By 2000, analysts realized that companies had huge commitments in the form of stock options to executives and employees, but these did not show up anywhere except in the footnotes. Also not reported was the diluting effect that these unrecorded liabilities had on the value of the stock held by the public. The slow-moving pace of reform in accounting rules meant that these huge stock option liabilities were not required to be reported until 2005.

3. *Commitments.* A footnote discussing a "commitment" may involve liabilities that have not been recorded on the balance sheet. There may be many justifications for these exclusions, including that accounting rules do not require them to be listed. When subsidiaries and partner-

ships are not consolidated into the balance sheet, the related liabilities are left off as well. So it is entirely possible for companies to have very large liabilities off the balance sheet. And, as Enron's example demonstrates, this has occurred in the past.

4. *Contingent liabilities.* A company may or may not owe money in the near future. Such "contingent" liabilities can arise from pending lawsuits, for example. The case of Merck and its contingent liabilities for Vioxx-related lawsuits includes potentially huge liabilities. As of January 1, 2005, the company was informed of 850 lawsuits pending, with 2,425 plaintiffs. In its 2004 annual report, Merck stated:

> Unfavorable outcomes in the *Vioxx* lawsuits or resulting from the *Vioxx* investigations could have a material adverse effect on the Company's financial position, liquidity and results of operations.[1]

The same footnote disclosed that the company had set up a $675 million reserve for its legal defense alone. In fairness to the company, it would not be realistic for it to recognize liabilities for any damages that might or might not result from litigation. The disclosure is substantial, and that is the point. On the one hand, no one would expect a company to record a liability that did not yet exist; on the other hand, if you were thinking about buying Merck stock, you would want to know about the 850 pending lawsuits and to review Merck's capital strength in light of those contingencies.

Key point: Contingent liabilities are disclosed in footnotes, but dollar values are not always included. It is often impossible to know in advance how much the contingency would cost the company.

The liabilities that you are likely to find off the balance sheet are not always minor; many of them, as in the case of Merck's pending litigation or GM's pension liabilities, are substantial. In some cases, these unrecorded liabilities exceed the company's total net worth.

Contingencies can also be found on the asset side of the balance sheet. For example, a company may be a plaintiff in a pending legal action, and the contingent receivable—which will become real only if and when the company wins the case—may have the same status as a contingent liability. When should this contingency be disclosed, how is it to be valued or discounted, and what effect will it have on *your* decision to buy or not to buy the stock? In any analysis of a company, it is wise to be aware of contingencies and their possible impact on valuation, even when you cannot assign a dollar value to them. In most situations, contingencies are likely to be found on the liability side, and, as in the case of Merck, the possible effect can be significant.

One troubling aspect of undisclosed liabilities is the effect that they may have on how ownership of stock is to be viewed. From the point of view of accounting firms and corporate management, if the public realized the extent of these liabilities, what would the consequences be? Just as the homeowner who discovered undisclosed liens would feel cheated, the stockholder might have a similar reaction. If accounting rules were changed suddenly, the possible reaction could be severe.

In 2002, General Electric announced that it was going to restate its financial results to expense employee stock options. (This did not become a *requirement* until three years later, so GE's decision was a bold one.) The company also reported that it was enacting a one-year holding period for option exercises by its senior management and a requirement that officers buy and hold stock on a salary-based formula.[2]

A year later, in 2003, Microsoft took a different course to solve the same problem of off-balance-sheet employee stock options. The company announced that it would no longer grant options to employees, but would begin granting shares to employees directly as an alternative. These incentives began to show up as expenses for the year in which stock was transferred.[3]

Key point: Although a handful of companies voluntarily reformed their stock option practices in 2002 and 2003, the *requirement* did not go into effect until 2005.

The GE and Microsoft changes were the beginnings of reform in the system that emerged throughout the 1990s, in which large commitments such as employee stock options simply vanished into the footnotes, and the liabilities were left off the balance sheet. The Financial Accounting Standards Board (FASB) announced near the end of 2004 that stock option grants were a type of compensation and should be shown as an expense (and a liability). This new rule went into effect as of 2005.[4]

Change takes time, as this ruling demonstrates. The ramifications are potentially severe, and so GAAP changes can adversely affect the perceived valuation of publicly listed companies. Standard & Poor's estimated, for example, that the change in the accounting treatment of employee stock options would reduce reported earnings for the S&P 500 companies by 7.4 percent in 2004.[5]

▲ UNDERVALUED ASSETS

The problems involving these core adjustments are not limited to unrecorded liabilities. Clearly, any unreported or distorted information presents a false picture of net worth, earnings power, and capital strength, and this can work in both directions. Just as liabilities can be underreported, so can assets. In the 1980s, Lucky Stores stock was bought up and the company was taken over. Why? Because someone recognized an opportunity for profit: The land owned by Lucky was worth more than the total of its capital stock. In the rapidly appreciating California market, this presented an opportunity during an era of leveraged buyouts.

> **Key point:** You cannot tell what real estate is worth by looking at the balance sheet. Valuation is reported at purchase price, *less* depreciation. This is anything but realistic, but it conforms to the accounting standards.

Why wasn't this fact obvious to everyone? The answer is found in the inaccuracies of financial reporting. Companies record assets at acquisition value and do not update these values even when the assets appreciate. On the contrary, accounting rules require companies to *reduce* the value of assets, even when their market value is rising.

Consider the example of a company that buys land and a building for $16 million. Let's assume that the land is worth $6 million and the improvements are worth $10 million. Both are recorded at the purchase price. Accounting rules state that the improvements are to be depreciated over 39 years. Land is not depreciated at all. Let's also assume that the market value of this property is rising by 8 percent per year. In this situation, the disparity between book value and market value becomes wider each year, as shown in Table 4.1.

Anyone who has followed the real estate markets will understand that a 10-year average increase in market value of 8 percent per year is realistic, especially in prime markets. This illustration shows the flaw in the accounting rules: While the book value of real estate declines from $16 million to $13.564 million over a decade, the market value more than doubles, to $34.543 million. This nearly $21 million of additional market value will not show up on the balance sheet but will be found only in the footnotes.

The example used a modestly priced $16 million building. In practice, large corporations own real estate worth far more. For example, as of its 2004 year-end, General Electric reported ownership of $19.2 billion in real estate, and Wal-Mart's 2005 annual statement showed $61.1 billion.[6]

These huge dollar values have been recorded under the same antiquated accounting rules used in the previous example. These were the

TABLE 4.1   CHANGES IN REAL ESTATE VALUES.

YEAR	Book Value			Total Market Value
	Land	Building	Total	
0	$ 6,000,000	$10,000,000	$16,000,000	$16,000,000
1	$ 6,000,000	$ 9,871,795	$15,871,795	$17,280,000
2	6,000,000	9,615,385	15,615,385	18,662,400
3	6,000,000	9,358,975	15,358,975	20,155,392
4	6,000,000	9,102,565	15,102,565	21,767,823
5	6,000,000	8,846,155	14,846,155	23,509,249
6	$ 6,000,000	$ 8,589,745	$14,589,745	$25,389,989
7	6,000,000	8,333,335	14,333,335	27,421,188
8	6,000,000	8,076,925	14,076,925	29,614,883
9	6,000,000	7,820,515	13,820,515	31,984,073
10	6,000,000	7,564,105	13,564,105	34,542,799

values of real estate at acquisition cost minus depreciation, *not* current market value. How much higher is current value than net book value? Of course, the higher the original cost of real estate and the longer the period of time that has passed, the greater the disparity between these two different valuations.

Analysts like to refer to tangible book value, which is shareholders' equity minus any intangible assets. This value may be far from realistic, as a result of the sum total of each year's accumulated exclusions of both assets and liabilities. Each year that expenses such as stock options were excluded, the retained earnings (part of net worth) was overstated. Each year that real estate is depreciated while market value rises, the asset value is understated. So the "book value per share" and "tangible book value" as reported may be far from the true values that investors need and want to see.

> **Key point:** If you rely on reported book value per share, you are probably relying on unrealistic and inaccurate numbers. And those numbers are blessed by the accounting industry.

These problems—exclusion of real and current values—can only be estimated by anyone outside of the corporation itself. You have no way to know the real market value of GE's or Wal-Mart's real estate, nor what liabilities are unrevealed on their balance sheets. Making the problem even worse, accounting rules allow these inaccuracies to pass for accurate reflections of value, even when accountants and corporate executives know better.

In picking stocks for investment based on fundamentals, the balance sheet is hopelessly out of date and provides no practical value. It is useful for tracking the short list of financial ratios, but that is all. You can judge and compare working capital and capitalization over time, and these are revealing statistical and fundamental indicators. But if you are inclined toward comparing book value or selecting stocks based on the dollar values of their assets or their total net worth, you also need to be aware of the shortcomings in current accounting rules.

With these flaws in mind, you may ignore ratios that compare operating statement results with balance sheet values. They are simply not reliable. Some analysts like to study return on investment, for example, dividing net earnings by the reported value of shareholders' equity. But because the equity valuation is entirely unreliable, such ratios provide a misleading picture. Using return on investment as a method for comparing investments is a distortion of reality because of the inaccuracies in the reported values of assets and liabilities on the balance sheet.

▲ CORE EARNINGS ADJUSTMENTS

The very idea that financial statements should be *accurate* often takes people by surprise. One group—including the average investor—is surprised and disturbed to learn that they do not already get accurate financial statements. The second group, including some corporate executives, Wall Street insiders, and accountants, is troubled at the problems that might arise if companies were required to reveal that (1) profits are vastly overstated and (2) the net worth of some corporations is much less than previously believed and in some instances may even be negative.

> **Key point:** Unless you adjust earnings to isolate the core business activity, you cannot accurately project likely future growth. The numbers include items that should be left out.

The decision by the FASB to require the inclusion of stock options as an expense beginning in 2005 caused widespread concern among insiders. For anyone who thinks that this is only a minor adjustment, remember the Associated Press story citing an adjustment to 2004 earnings of over 7 percent among S&P 500 companies. This level of restatement is huge, and it threatens the foundations of what many insiders and investors have come to believe.

> **How the numbers work.** Imagine going to your bank to apply for a loan. You sold your home last year and made a profit of $250,000. You also earned an $80,000 salary last year. On your loan application, you list your "annual income" as $330,000. Your banker is impressed at first, but soon realizes that you in-

cluded your capital gain, which is promptly removed. You're told that you cannot include the profit from the sale of your home as income.

Although that rule makes sense, this is exactly what corporations do every year when they report to stockholders results other than their core earnings. Under GAAP rules, no such adjustments are required to be made *or* disclosed on the financial statement itself.

The source of inaccuracy involves core earnings, those earnings derived strictly from the core product or service that the company markets. Core earnings are different from reported net earnings because of the specific inclusions of noncore items in reported net earnings and exclusions of core expenses. Adjustments are needed to arrive at core earnings, and these are found in the corporate footnotes. They include the following six:

1. *Nonrecurring income.* The "net earnings," which include nonoperating (and noncore) items, should be adjusted, and net *operating* profit should be used for all calculations. Nonrecurring income includes income from the sale of capital assets, receipts growing out of litigation, insurance settlements, and other one-time nonrecurring or so-called extraordinary items. These adjustments may be in either direction. For example, if a company makes a profit from selling capital assets, that profit is supposed to be removed. A loss, in comparison, is added back to arrive at core earnings.

2. *Accounting adjustments and revaluations.* The way in which companies set up inventory values, reserves, or the timing for booking revenues, costs, and expenses is supposed to be consistent each year, but these valuations may be changed as a result of new interpretations of the law, new accounting opinions, or new laws. But the resulting effect on profit or loss should be excluded in a core earnings study.

3. *The sale of corporate segments.* When companies make profits by selling off segments of their operations, current and historical earnings should be restated to exclude the earnings that were derived from those segments. For example, in 2002, Altria sold off its Miller Beer segment

and received $2.6 billion.[7] Two adjustments have to be made. First, 2002 net earnings should be adjusted downward by $2.6 billion to exclude the sold-off segment. Second, historical revenues and earnings have to be adjusted downward so that past and current earnings can be tracked realistically to judge how future earnings will be likely to emerge.

4. *Merger and acquisition changes.* When companies merge or acquire other companies, the entire financial picture changes. To ensure historical accuracy, the operating statements have to be restated as though the companies had been together for the entire historical period being studied. A related noncore item is the amortization of acquisition costs. This is a complex area of accounting, and the accounting gimmicks of the 1990s included many examples of profits created artificially by the treatment of mergers and acquisitions, and by the timing for booking or writing off reserves related to those accounting changes.

5. *Expenses excluded from the GAAP statements.* Any expenses that are not included in the normal operating statement should be added back in. These are normally found in the footnotes. To some, it would seem extraordinary that corporations would fail to include and deduct expenses, and even more so that accountants would allow that practice. But even though the practice of excluding often substantial employee stock options was known for many years, including these as expenses was not a requirement until 2005. Even then the change was controversial.

6. *Pension asset pro forma profits.* A potentially large core earnings adjustment involves future profits from the investment of pension assets. These *pro forma* earnings have to be taken out of the reported earnings of the company. In the past, the inclusion of the estimated profit was approved under GAAP, but its accuracy is questionable. In practice, there is no assurance that investments will make any profits; they may even lose money. So pro forma income should be taken out of the reported earnings as a core earnings adjustment.

"For the sake of form." That is what *pro forma* means. In accounting, pro forma statements are a device for projecting and forecasting budgets or for estimating profits from future activity. Pro forma earnings are questionable because assumptions can be made to look more promising than reality.

Making these adjustments does not mean that the profit and loss from noncore activities does not count. It only means that the dollar amount should be excluded from the annual statement-based analysis of financial trends in revenues and earnings.

▲ CORE EARNINGS AND THE EFFECT ON OTHER RATIOS

The adjustments made to increase or decrease reported profits will affect the ratios you use in your analysis of the financial parts of the annual report. The effect on balance sheet ratios may be minimal, although the changes will affect capitalization to some degree. The higher the core earnings adjustments are, the greater the impact they have. But by far the greater impact of core earnings adjustments will be seen in ratios involving the operating statement, such as net return. The P/E ratio will also be affected. These two ratios—net return and P/E—are likely to be the ones most affected as a result of making core earnings adjustments. They also are the two most popular ratios investors use.

> **Key point:** To make any ratio reliable and accurate, you need to ensure that its components are accurate. For this reason, you need to use *core* earnings as well as asset and liability values.

For many reasons, the fact that it is necessary to adjust the numbers is scandalous. Investors judge the potential for growth in investment value based on earnings and P/E, so at the very least, everyone should be concerned about differences between these ratios when they are calculated using the GAAP-approved statements and those calculated using the core earnings–adjusted results.

In studying annual reports, you cannot expect corporate officers or the auditors to provide you with interpretive information. As the concept of transparency develops over time, the day may come when that occurs, but for now you need to make your own adjustments in order to ensure the quality of the ratios you use. The information you need to make core earnings adjustments is found in the footnotes. The most important of these adjustments include the removal of pro forma pension income, gains from selling assets or corporate segments, and accounting adjustments that will not recur in the future. All of this information can be located in the footnotes, as explained in chapters 5 and 6.

Two revised ratios will prove valuable to you in your analysis and comparison of corporate financial results. These are *core* net return and *core* P/E.

The core net return is calculated using the operating profit, adjusted for all the core earnings changes that you discover in a study of the footnotes. A comparison between net return and core net return may be revealing. Ideally, a well-run corporation should not experience a high level of core earnings adjustments. A high level of such adjustments might indicate that the corporation has, in fact, been manipulating the numbers to create a desired financial outcome. It is not proof, but it could be one of many signs. The troubling fact that some manipulation is allowed under GAAP makes the point that high levels of adjustments point to trouble.

Tracking core net return is more reliable than tracking net return without these adjustments. The potential for long-term growth is always going to be based on core numbers, not on overall unadjusted numbers that include nonrecurring elements. Remember, the unadjusted net profits distort results and cannot be relied upon. Table 4.2 demonstrates the problem and its possible scope, comparing net earnings and core earnings for four companies.

These summaries of IBM, Boeing, Altria Corporation, and Ford Motor Company show the results for the four years between 2001 and 2004. (Standard & Poor's invented the concept of core earnings and first applied it in fiscal year 2001.) Some years show upward adjustments, but most of the adjustments are downward. For IBM, the most drastic occurred in 2001 and 2002, when more than $5 billion in downward adjustments was required. Of the four companies selected, these were the most drastic differences between net and core earnings.

Key point: For some corporations, substantial core earnings adjustments—$5 billion or more—are required to arrive at accurate earnings numbers.

TABLE 4.2   CORE EARNINGS ADJUSTMENTS.[1]

Company	In millions of dollars			
	2004	2003	2002	2001
IBM				
Net Earnings[2]	8,448	7,613	5,334	7,723
Core Earnings[3]	6,923	5,270	111	2,302
Boeing				
Net Earnings	1,820	718	492	2,827
Core Earnings	1,616	1,074	203	284
Altria				
Net Earnings	9,420	9,204	11,102	8,566
Core Earnings	9,348	9,145	8,593	7,959
Ford				
Net Earnings	3,634	921	284	(5,453)
Core Earnings	3,637	1,905	(2,202)	(8,266)

1. *Source:* Standard & Poor's Stock Reports, December 2005; at web site of Charles Schwab & Sons, http:/investing.schwab.com.
2. Net earnings after taxes.
3. "Core earnings" as developed and defined by Standard & Poor's.

While the result recommended for use in ratios is the net operating earnings, these examples use net earnings to demonstrate the drastic differences when core earnings adjustments are made, as many such adjustments show up in the "other" categories between operating income and net income. The large changes shown for companies like IBM also affect the EPS and, as a direct result, the core P/E.

A billion versus a million. How much is a billion? If a million dollars requires a stack of $100 bills five feet high, a similar stack for a billion dollars would have to be nearly one *mile* high.

The extent of core earnings adjustments cannot be known until an analysis is done. Because the S&P Stock Reports present the adjusted figures for you, they are an exceptionally valuable resource for core earnings adjustments. Finding precise footnotes, interpreting them, and making the dollar adjustments is complex. The S&P Stock Reports make it easier.

Valuable Resource: The S&P Stock Reports are available from many online brokerage services. Because these services do not charge a subscription fee, the stock reports offered by specific sites are free as well. Charles Schwab & Co. (http: investing.schwab.com) is probably the best-known online site offering this free service.

▲ RECALCULATING A CORPORATION'S CORE NET WORTH

Besides watching and tracking revenues and earnings, investors also follow a company's balance sheet and its capitalization, net worth, and working capital trends. However, if core earnings adjustments are significant, so are changes in core net worth.

By definition, *core* net worth is the true net worth when a balance sheet's assets and liabilities are adjusted to their true values. You cannot remove core earnings adjustments from reported net worth, however. In reality, the net income reported on the operating statement is a verifiable and real number, even though core earnings adjustments have not been made. For example, when Altria sold Miller Beer in 2002, its core earnings had to be adjusted by $2.6 billion. But the company did receive that money, and it does properly belong in the retained earnings for the year 2002.

Core net worth is, instead, the result of changes made to asset and liability accounts. These adjustments include adding liabilities for off-balance-sheet obligations like long-term leases and estimates for contingent liabilities. It is difficult to assign a tangible value to contingencies because no one can know ahead of time whether those liabilities will become real or not and, if they do, what the dollar amount might be. Merck is a good example; the contingent liability for hundreds of pending lawsuits is staggering, but assigning a value to that contingency is impossible. So in adjusting the core net worth, some estimates are going to be required. At the very least, net worth has to be qualified with an awareness of the contingency.

Key point: You are not always able to assign a value to a contingency. But at the very least, any judgments you make about a company's financial health should include an awareness of that contingency.

Moving the net worth in the opposite direction is the potentially large adjustment to reflect the fair market value of real estate. The accounting rules require that real estate be depreciated, so that each year's net book value declines. However, it is possible and often probable that real estate values will rise. For example, Wal-Mart reported real estate at the end of 2004 in excess of $60 billion book value. What is the *market value* of that real estate?

In a completely transparent form of reporting, companies would disclose their results in three distinct formats: GAAP, statutory, and core. The GAAP format, the only one you normally have the chance to see in the annual report, is seriously flawed and does not present a true picture. The inaccuracies of asset and liability valuation are only one problem; the differences between net earnings and *core* net earnings at times run into the billions. As a consequence, when you discover through the news that General Motors would be bankrupt if it booked its current pension liabilities, it comes as a surprise because GAAP does not require these liabilities to be included.

The second format, statutory, would be what companies report to the IRS and state taxing authorities. This is often far different from what you see in the annual report. The tax-based reporting is rarely shown to investors. The earnings may be much lower on a statutory basis than in a GAAP-based report.

The third format would adjust asset, liability, and net worth values to reflect a realistic basis for net worth. This may be defined as "what the company would be worth if it were offered for sale." This is an ironic definition, because companies are actually "sold" every day through publicly exchanged stock, where the price per share is almost always far above book value. But using the market value of assets and the true obligations for known liabilities would make corporate balance sheets look vastly different from the GAAP format.

While this three-part financial report is not likely to become the norm in the near future, it would certainly be an enlightened change. The call for transparency has been largely given lip service following the period of corporate scandals. Conflicts of interest remain, and annual reports continue to offer only a passive rendition of the numbers.

Chapters 5 and 6 delve into a complex area of the annual report: the footnotes. These technically complex explanations of financial results could be made simpler, but in many respects the entire annual report is more of a *legal* document than an educational one. As with other forms of transparency, the long-term trend may be toward more understandable disclosure formats and explanations. For now, it is necessary to dissect the footnotes in stages, and to seek specific interpretations.

CHAPTER 5

FOOTNOTES, PART 1

AN OVERVIEW OF THE *REAL* DISCLOSURES

The footnotes section of the annual report takes up more room than all the other sections combined. The complexity of these notes—which often exceed 100 pages—is a result of the complexity of accounting itself, the broad range of topics that have to be covered, and the nature of many large corporations, whose diversified holdings often include numerous different types of operations.

Consider the case of Altria, one of dozens of companies whose annual reports were analyzed for this chapter. The company (better known as Philip Morris and trading under the symbol MO) has one of the most accessible and easy-to-use web sites among larger corporations. Its company includes the following operating units: Philip Morris USA, Philip Morris International, Kraft Foods, and Philip Morris Capital. Beyond tobacco operations, Kraft Foods alone has a large number of subsidiaries and product lines, such as DiGiorno, Nabisco, Lunchables, Ritz Crackers, Jell-O, South Beach Products, Oreo Cookies, Tang, Philadelphia Cream Cheese, Oscar Mayer, Capri Sun, Planters Peanuts, Kool-Aid, Gevelia Coffee, Sanka, Tombstone Pizza, Shake 'n Bake, Cream of Wheat, Dream Whip, Post Cereals, Minute Rice, Barnum's Animal Crackers, and Life Savers candy—to name a few. In fact, Kraft has its own web site and annual report under its umbrella as a subsidiary of Altria.

This company is highlighted not to promote its product line but to make an important point: Many large, diversified corporations have complex reporting demands. The differences in reported profitability between domestic and international tobacco products and food and household items is significant.

▲ FOOTNOTE BASICS

In this chapter, the footnotes of typical annual reports are highlighted. The examples and descriptions of footnotes are typical but not necessarily all-inclusive. Corporations tend to include many of the same footnotes or to cover the same topics but under different names. The original purpose of footnotes was to augment the information in the financial statements. For example, a one-line total for "expenses" would be supported with a footnote explaining the details, or changes in reserves for bad debts, inventory valuation, or capital assets would be discussed more broadly in a narrative section. This enables the company to report the numbers in a summarized format and discuss those numbers in detail in its footnotes.

Key point: The footnotes provide support for the summarized numerical information in financial statements. This detail fosters understanding of the importance of the statements, what they reveal, and what is left off them.

This original purpose of the footnotes has not changed. But it has been broadened as a result of regulatory requirements, new laws regarding disclosure, and the complexity of larger, publicly listed, diversified organizations. The area of mergers, acquisitions, and divestitures (sales) of operating segments—and the resulting effect on the financial statements—is especially complex. In fact, one of the recurring problems found in many companies involved in the corporate scandals (the Enron age) was the misuse of acquisitions to artificially bolster earnings. During the 1990s, companies like Sysco, Waste Management, and Cendant/CUC bolstered their earnings through dozens of acquisitions, creation of partnerships or subsidiaries, and the use of questionable accounting practices. The leader in this abuse, of course, was Enron, which was estimated to have created over 3,000 partnerships and "special-purpose entities." These complex matters are not easy to find, and, as the past has revealed, companies do not always tell the truth about them in their annual reports. If you have found yourself uncertain about what you can glean from these reports, you are not alone. Even the Dow Jones Company, a widely acknowledged expert on the stock market, was fooled by Enron. Dow Jones, which publishes the well-known market averages, included Enron in the Dow Jones Utility Average until the truth about Enron's deceptions became widely known.

When corporations do everything aboveboard, footnotes are important documents that explain and disclose matters for shareholders, analysts, and regulators. They may be prepared by the corporation or by the team of outside auditors, and in most instances the collection of footnotes is added to both internally and as part of the audit. So the footnotes are a complex series of explanations, even for experienced accountants.

When corporations set out to deceive investors, inflate earnings, and create artificial growth in the stock price—as Enron and many others did—the footnotes can be used to complicate matters and to confuse rather than to clarify.

Footnotes are necessary because of the underlying complexity of financial reporting. In big companies like Altria or IBM, for example, many circumstances have to be explained in detail, including everything from accounting policies to segment information, income tax liabilities, and retirement plan accounting. Investors often have a tendency to treat footnotes as being so complex that it is impossible to make sense of them, and so simply fail to read them at all. At the very least, investors should skim over the footnotes to try to find important details. For example, looking at Altria's overall revenues, it is difficult to tell where actual growth has occurred. In its 2004 statement, the company reported *falling* operating earnings over three years:

2004	$14.004 BILLION
2003	14.609 BILLION
2002	17.945 BILLION

What does this reveal? In checking the company's footnote on segment information, explanations for the earnings decline are found. In 2002, the company's profits included the sale of its Miller Beer segment for $2.6 billion, plus 2002 operating revenue of $276 million for that segment. So a total of over $2.9 billion derived from the Miller segment does not show up again in 2003 or 2004. In addition, revenues from domestic tobacco operations declined over the three years.

> **Key point:** One purpose of the footnotes is to provide detailed explanation that it is not practical or possible to provide in a one-page financial statement.

Analyzing a company's results by segment often reveals the real underlying trends, whereas trends in companywide results—a combination of often contradictory trends—may not be easy to follow. In fact, some apparent trends can be easily explained, as in the Altria example. Collectively, annual revenues and profits are remarkably consistent when the sold-off segment is excluded from the numbers.

Footnotes can clarify the numbers, enabling more intelligent analysis. In addition, they are useful for additional types of analysis. A highly detailed core earnings adjustment process is possible using the footnotes. (However, Standard & Poor's provides summarized core earnings values in its stock reports, which saves a lot of time.) You can also use the footnotes to better understand the company's long-term liabilities, its contingencies and commitments (off-balance-sheet liabilities), and the acquisition and sale of capital assets.

A valuable feature of many—but not all—annual reports is the inclusion of contact information. For example, Altria includes "Shareholder Information" as a section of its annual report, listing contact names and numbers for its home office and a Shareholder Response Center complete with toll-free phone number. IBM's "Stockholder Information" section includes similar resource and contact information. And GE's annual report ends with a "Corporate Information" section including Shareholder Services contact information.

These departments within a company are responsible for answering questions about the company's financial reports. If particular footnotes do not make sense or if you have questions about any section of the annual report or a company's financial statements, contacting the company directly is a sensible course of action. A helpful and enlightened response is always refreshing. By the same argument, a dismissive reply, no reply, or a reply that only confuses you more is a sign that the company does not understand the importance of helping shareholders, analysts, and the general public. The majority of shareholder services departments will be as responsive as possible and can help to clarify the annual report's footnotes.

Key point: The shareholder service departments of corporations exist primarily to answer your questions. The tone of this department's response to your phone call and the level of service it offers are factors that you can use for selecting stocks.

In the following sections, the most common footnotes are explained. You may find additional notes, and not very company will have all of these footnotes. And while virtually every annual report gives footnotes as a single section, this discussion attempts to classify footnotes. There is no established sequence for footnotes, either, so reading through them can be disorienting and confusing. In the following sections, 34 commonly found footnotes are explained in detail; companies often include nonrecurring footnotes in addition to these, and the actual corporate footnotes may also be given different names. Most of the examples are derived from the annual reports for Altria Corporation and IBM for the year 2004. These two companies were selected because both of them have exceptionally complex business situations, reflected in their footnotes, and both have excellent web sites. The annual reports for both of these companies are examples of complex but well-presented annual report information.

▲ VALUATION FOOTNOTES

Footnotes often begin with an overview note that explains the background and scope of the financial statements. For example, companies with diversified segments may need to explain that the consolidated statements include (1) a mix of dissimilar product and service lines and geographically based subsidiaries, (2) restated revenues and earnings resulting from acquisitions, mergers, or sales of major segments, and (3) the effects of restatements due to accounting changes and other major impacts.

This *background and basis* footnote (as Altria Corporation names it) is valuable in that it expresses the premises and assumptions under which the statements were prepared. Altria breaks the note into two specific parts. In the "background" section, Altria identifies its five major operating companies (holding company, domestic tobacco, international tobacco, Kraft Foods, and its leasing subsidiary). It also explains that Miller Brewing was sold in 2002 and is excluded from historical data in a restated format. In the "basis of presentation" section, the company explains the accounting methods it uses. It also includes a notice that the financial statements conform to GAAP principles. And finally, it discloses restatements resulting from discontinued operations.

Most companies' annual report footnotes do not present this background and basis footnote, and that is unfortunate. Instead, the explanation of these essential accounting and presentation facts is sprinkled throughout various footnotes and in other sections of the annual report. For anyone who sits down and begins reading through the dozens of pages of footnotes, the orientation provided through a background and basis footnote is very useful.

> **Key point:** Providing the reader with an initial footnote that provides a broad overview is an excellent start. Unfortunately, few companies go to the trouble of writing this essential first footnote.

Virtually all annual reports include a footnote called *significant accounting policies*. This note can be very technical, as it includes disclosures of the accounting decisions affecting the valuation of assets as well as methods used in recording revenues, costs, and expenses. While these disclosures have to be provided, it is not always clear how the specific policies affect profitability. Some examples of the types of accounting policies you will find here are:

Cash and cash equivalents. This is an explanation of what is included in the current asset Cash. For example, it may include cash deposits plus short-term investments maturing within a few months.

Depreciation. The company depreciates assets using one of several allowed methods, and there are usually distinct differences between the GAAP-reported depreciation expense and the amount reported for tax purposes.

Goodwill and other intangible assets. The treatment of intangible assets, those without physical value, includes the methods used to amortize (write off) those assets over time. Goodwill is the value of a company's market reputation; other intangible assets may include brand names, trademarks, or licenses and can have considerable value.

Currency exchange. The company may report income or expense arising from differences in currency exchange rates. This section explains how the valuation for the date of the financial statement is arrived at.

Hedging instrument valuation. Assets are often invested in options and other derivative instruments. This is included here to explain how these holdings are valued at the statement date.

Asset impairment. Some assets lose value over time in a way that is not otherwise reported under strict basis and depreciation rules. Whenever the current value of assets is lower than the net book value, impairment has to be reported under GAAP rules.

Valuation sections. Accounting valuation decisions can have a major impact on earnings, especially in two areas: income taxes and inventory. Deferred taxes can be computed in different ways, and companies have to conform to the prescribed GAAP methods for determining future liabilities. Inventory valuation can be based on the lower of cost or market, and specific valuation decisions affect the cost of goods sold.

Revenue recognition. The timing of revenue recognition is specifically explained here. Normally, revenue is booked when goods are shipped to customers. The method used on the financial statements is explained.

Stock-based compensation. Companies have historically included stock options as part of a compensation package, especially for executives, but until 2005 there was no requirement that they report this compensation. Thus, when stock options were exercised, the overall value of shares was diluted, but the expense was never reported. The methods used for granting options are explained here. For example, some companies (such as General Electric) require employees to hold options for a minimum period and to maintain a specified level of stock ownership as part of a stock-based ownership agreement.

Restructuring costs. The term *restructuring* is a technical phrase that usually means cutting costs. Plants may be closed and consolidated, lines of products phased out, and jobs eliminated. These changes involve costs, and the accounting for those costs is explained here.

Key point: Many annual reports have numerous "significant" policies to report. The complexity and scope of these policies may reflect rule changes or internal changes in the company itself.

Some companies isolate specific types of accounting matters in a note called *accounting changes.* For example, IBM includes a separate note to explain how it values stock-based compensation and derivatives and when it recognizes revenues, among other topics. So it is possible to have two or more notes covering accounting matters or to isolate significant accounting policies and accounting changes in separate notes. The decision may be based on the complexity of the accounting decisions in a particular year.

Accounting-based footnotes are complex not only because companies make decisions in a technical environment, but also because the rules change. Each year the Financial Accounting Standards Board (FASB) issues new rulings or opinions, and companies must revise their previous policies to conform to these rules. The FASB moves slowly, but its changes are part of a reform and improvement movement within the industry. For example, its ruling requiring the reporting of stock options as current expenses led to the need for a footnote regarding accounting changes for all companies using stock-based plans. Significant changes are not always designed by corporations or accounting firms, but may be required by the accounting industry and its regulators.

▲ ASSET FOOTNOTES

A series of footnotes explains valuation and changes in various asset accounts. The first is *accounts receivable*, the value of amounts due from sales made on credit, adjusted downward for reserves for bad debts. In this footnote, changes in accounts receivable are explained (this may also include any notes receivable). A lot of attention is also paid to bad debts. Bad debt expense is usually recorded as an addition to a *reserve* for bad debts, an asset account that reduces accounts receivable.

Some companies include a related footnote for the *sale of receivables*. The organization may sell receivables to another company to improve its cash flow. For example, in a footnote to its 2004 annual report titled "Sale and Securitization of Receivables," IBM reported that it sold trade receivables in exchange for a servicing fee. The receivables sold under this plan are also pledged as collateral for some forms of borrowing.

Key point: Not every company needs every type of footnote. For example, while some companies sell their accounts receivable, most do not.

Careful attention should be paid to how companies value their *inventories*. The footnote on this topic provides a simple two-year or three-year comparison of changes in inventory levels, if no significant changes in valuation methods were made during the year. No comments were included in IBM's inventory footnote for 2004; in the case of Altria, no annual comparisons were shown in the footnote, but the company did explain the valuation method it used.

A footnote for *properties and depreciation* (which may also have other titles, such as "Property, Plant, and Equipment" or "Long-Term Assets") describes these assets' value and changes in value, often with a two-year comparison of changes. IBM's 2004 footnote "Plant, Rental Machines and Other Property" includes a two-year summary in three asset classifications, less depreciation; rental assets less depreciation; and a net total.

Changes in ownership of segments involve two footnotes, usually titled *acquisitions* and *divestitures*. When a company acquires a new segment, the details are explained in the "Acquisitions" footnote. For example, Altria's 2004 acquisitions included the purchase by Kraft Foods of a beverage operation in Finland, a planned acquisition of a large tobacco business in Colombia, and purchases of tobacco businesses in Serbia and Greece. Kraft also had new operations in Egypt, Australia, and Turkey. IBM's 2004 annual report listed 14 separate acquisitions and several divestures (explained in the same footnote), along with charts showing the purchase and sale values.

Altria reported its divestitures in a separate footnote (IBM put acquisitions and divestitures together). In Altria's case, the company reported a significant sale: Kraft's sugar confectionary operation was sold for $1.5 billion. (This included Life Savers and Altoids, among other products.)

In all cases of acquisitions and divestitures, the current and historical results have to be restated. In complex organizations such as Altria and IBM, it is likely that a number of acquisitions and divestitures will occur every year, so accounting for these changes is complex. From the typical investor's point of view, these changes also affect the calculation of core earnings. Because long-term growth potential changes every time a company acquires another company or sells a segment, this calculation is necessary every year.

Another of the asset footnotes is *financial instruments*. Most corporations invest their excess cash in derivatives, money market instruments, foreign currencies, and other short-term products to create income until that cash is required for operations. Of concern to investors and analysts is the level of risk that companies take when they use their cash for short-term investing. Besides disclosing where funds are invested and how those levels have changed from year to year, this footnote also explains how these financial instruments were valued on the balance sheet. Normally, they would be reported at the fair market value at the closing date for the annual report. In some cases (such as Altria's), the footnote provides a detailed discussion with explanations of total asset values. In the IBM annual report, a chart is included listing marketable securities by classification, with only a single paragraph discussing financial instruments. While Altria goes to great lengths to explain its policies for selection of risk and valuation of financial instruments, IBM simply states that its financial instruments are reported at fair market value.

A final asset-related footnote discusses *intangible assets*. In some cases, such as Altria's 2004 annual report, the important details concerning valuation and amortization of intangibles are included in the note on significant accounting policies. In others, as in IBM's annual report for 2004, a detailed note "Intangible Assets Including Goodwill" provides numerous details and comparative charts breaking down many classifications of intangible assets and their valuation, amortization, and changes from one year to the next. Because IBM's business involves so many intellectual property rights, numerous intangible assets are listed, such as capitalized software, completed technology, strategic alliances, and patents and trademarks—all in addition to goodwill.

The nature of intangibility. Many large corporations have high-value intangible assets. By definition, an "intangible" asset has no physical properties. This is why one key ratio comparing a company's book value to the number of shares outstanding excludes intangible assets. The *tangible book value per share* ignores intangible assets, even when they are very real and have actual value (such as brand names, trademarks, and so on).

▲ LIABILITY AND NET WORTH FOOTNOTES

There are also footnotes describing and explaining *short-term borrowings*. Some companies combine current accounts payable with other current liabilities and describe all current liabilities in one footnote. For example, Kodak provided a 2004 footnote in its annual statement called "Payables and Short-Term Borrowings." Most companies do not bother with explanatory footnotes for current accounts payable, but do provide details of short-term debt and the interest rates being paid. Altria's "Short-Term Borrowings and Borrowing Arrangements" footnote includes year-end

average rates plus narrative explanations for the Altria group and, separately, for Kraft Foods. IBM combines short-term and long-term debt in
the footnote "Borrowings." The short-term portion simply explains the
weighted-average interest rate on different types of borrowings and provides a two-year balance comparison. Providing more or less detail is not
an indication of whether the company has disclosed *enough* information.
The decision about how much narrative and financial detail to provide
depends on the circumstances and on the judgment of the auditors and
management.

> **Key point:** Most annual reports don't provide footnotes for
> current liabilities beyond short-term borrowings. These are usu-
> ally self-explanatory. When such footnotes are provided, it
> could signal some type of exceptional accounting treatment that
> is worth analyzing.

In *long-term borrowings*, a company usually provides far more detail,
especially when bond issues are part of the mix. Investors and analysts
have a keen interest in tracking long-term debt trends because capitalization is one of the most important indicators you can track. Altria's
"Long-Term Debt" footnote includes a two-year side-by-side comparison
in great detail, including notes, debentures (unsecured bonds), foreign
currency obligations, and bonds issued, shown by maturity year. IBM
provides a similar highly detailed summary, including a breakdown of
debentures by interest rate. Both Altria and IBM include brief narrative
explanations of debts, lines of credit, and interest rates.

Corporations may need to provide additional information concerning *other long-term liabilities*. For example, IBM offers a footnote called
"Other Liabilities" that includes a two-year summary of deferred taxes,
deferred income, executive compensation accruals, and other liabilities,
and an extensive explanation of these other liabilities and changes in balances from the past year to the latest year.

One of the more complex footnotes is *commitments and contingencies*.
In this footnote, you find disclosures of liabilities that are not shown on
the balance sheet and also of contingent liabilities (defined as potential
debts that might or might not become actual liabilities in the future).

IBM's annual report is fairly typical for a large corporation. Its contingencies explanation takes up slightly more than two pages in its 2004 annual report, and it includes explanations of the major cases in which the company was named as defendant along with estimates of legal costs to defend those cases. Contingencies also include its commitments under existing lines of credit, indemnifications that the company has made on behalf of other companies, and loan guarantees.

Altria has a far more complex situation, because of its pending tobacco litigation. In fact, its "Contingencies" footnote in 2004 takes up six full pages and exceeds 7,000 words. Subsections include an overview of tobacco-related litigation, complete with a chart showing a three-year summary of pending cases classified by type of case (individual smoking and health cases outnumber all others), pending and upcoming trials, recent trial results, class action suits, health-care recovery cost litigation and settlements, federal litigation, and special-category litigation. The footnote explains the potential liability level for each category. The complexity of tobacco-related litigation deserves such detailed treatment and will continue to do so for many years to come. This is and should be a major portion of the disclosures in Altria's annual report.

Key point: When a contingencies section is exceptionally long, it could signify future negative impacts on profitability. The tobacco and drug industries are especially vulnerable to lawsuits, and other industries may show the same trend in future reports.

All corporations explain their *stockholders' equity and capital stock* balances and changes from one year to the next in a specialized footnote. IBM's "Stockholders' Equity Activity" footnote contains narrative sections for stock repurchase plans (in which the company purchases and retires common stock, which then becomes permanently classified as "treasury stock" in the company books) and for gains or losses from nonoperational sources such as foreign currency, pension liabilities, and financial instruments. Altria's "Capital Stock" footnote for 2004 showed a two-year summary of common stock balances and changes during the year (new issues, repurchases, and exercise of stock options).

▲ OPERATING STATEMENT FOOTNOTES

The study of revenues, costs and expenses, and earnings forms the basis of most fundamental programs, and for good reason. Most investors want to buy stock in companies whose revenues and earnings are growing. When corporate history reaches a growth plateau, stock prices tend to do the same. Because the detailed study of these realities is so crucial to the investing decision, *segment information* is informative and valuable.

This is especially true when a corporate umbrella covers many diversified subsidiaries and operations. The economic and market factors for these segments may be dissimilar, and the reasonable expectations of earnings may differ as well. The range of likely earnings in various industries is substantial. For example, compare historical net return in the construction, retail, and computer software industries. It is important to study revenue and earnings trends by segment to gain a clear understanding of how trends are moving. If you look only at the overall, consolidated results, you may not recognize the trends in the mix.

> **Key point:** The summary of segment information reported by different companies should provide uniform information and report the same number of years. This is necessary to make intelligent comparisons.

Altria's 2004 annual report includes the footnote "Segment Reporting." IBM's corresponding footnote is called "Segment Information." Both contain the same types of information. Altria reported on five distinct segments (domestic tobacco, international tobacco, North American food, international food, and financial services). It also included the beer segment sold in 2002 as part of its three-year report. IBM's three-year reporting included three major segments (global services, hardware, and software) and several smaller ones. Both companies broke down revenue and earnings for a three-year period by segment. Both companies also reported their asset values, depreciation, and capital expenditures for the three years, broken down by segment.

A specialized footnote for the cost of *restructuring* may also appear in the annual report. In 2004, neither Altria nor IBM included a footnote of this type. However, Kodak devoted six pages of its 2004 annual report's footnotes to "Restructuring Costs." At the beginning of this lengthy footnote, an explanation is provided:

> Currently, the company is being adversely impacted by the progressing digital substitution. As the company continues to adjust its operating model in light of changing business conditions, it is probable that ongoing cost reduction activities will be required from time to time.

For the most part, this series of programs involves terminating employees and paying severance packages. Kodak, whose long history has been based on film, has been slow to make adjustments to the realities of digital technology—thus the extensive adjustments. While Kodak's restructuring programs emphasize reductions in its workforce, other forms of restructuring costs can include consolidation of plants and facilities, changes and improvements to internal controls, and cancellation of obligations (leases and other contracts). All of these forms of restructuring involve costs but are designed to provide longer-term cost and expense reductions.

Key point: You run into a lot of cloaked language in accounting. For example, "restructuring" is often a softer way of describing layoffs of employees to cut costs.

An especially complex footnote involves the discussion of *retirement plans*. This may also be called "Retirement-Related Benefits" (IBM), "Benefit Plans" (Altria), or any of a number of other variations. This is invariably a technical and complex footnote, and one that involves a lot of controversy. It includes a chart showing U.S. and non-U.S. costs, benefits, and other factors for various plan formats (defined-benefit plans, defined-contribution plans, and nonretirement benefit costs, for example). It also breaks down plan assets and explains accounting policies. A three-year chart explains the details and changes in costs and income. However, the stated value of "expected income" is considered a noncore item and is excluded from core earnings in the analysis performed by Standard & Poor's. The adjustments involving benefit plans may be the largest core earnings adjustment in the S&P summary (see S&P Stock Reports to compare GAAP earnings and core earnings).

Additionally, under current GAAP rules, companies are not required to show the full dollar value of plan obligations, which is lunacy. This is the primary reason that many big corporations such as United Airlines filed for bankruptcy protection in recent years; they cannot afford to pay the benefits that are contractually owed under their benefit plans. But these changes came as a surprise to many investors because the true scope of pension liabilities is not shown on the balance sheet.

Footnotes are also included for *specific expense categories* when a company believes that information on these expenses needs to be disclosed. For example, in 2004, IBM included footnotes for advertising and promotional expenses, and for research, development, and engineering expenses. Altria provided no additional expense-based footnotes.

A footnote for *stock options and compensation plans* involves a range of explanations for the incentive compensation that the company provides to board members, executives, and employees. IBM and Altria (in its note "Stock Plans") cover the same ground. The note includes an explanation of the scope of the incentives that the company provides. For example, IBM discusses stock option grants and employee stock option purchase plans; Altria provides explanations of employee stock options, stock appreciation rights, restricted stock, and incentive awards. Both companies, like virtually all companies that offer stock options, include a chart giving a three-year summary of the number of shares covered by options:

At the beginning of the year

Plus: options granted

Less: options exercised

Less: options canceled

At the end of the year

As of 2005, companies are required to show stock option expenses in the operating statement, which was not required previously. This new requirement may change the format of how options are reported in the footnotes in future annual reports.

Key point: With the changes in the reporting of stock option expenses in 2005, many companies may change the format of their corresponding footnote. At the very least, companies will have to restate past earnings to take this major change into account.

Another note explains activity and changes in *income taxes*. The format for reporting tax liabilities is fairly standard. Both IBM ("Taxes") and Altria ("Income Taxes") provide a three-year summary showing income before taxes; federal, state and local, and foreign tax liabilities; and the net earnings after taxes. A second chart provides a two-year explanation of deferred tax assets and liabilities. (Tax benefits and expenses are often deferred as a result of the capitalization of some types of expenses for tax but not GAAP accounting or vice versa, to be written off over several years.)

▲ OTHER TYPES OF FOOTNOTES

An important disclosure that serves to update information in the annual report is found in the footnote *subsequent events*. Different names may be used, but essentially this footnote advises of significant changes that occurred after the date of the annual report, but were known before its preparation was completed.

Delays of up to three months . . . or more. A company's fiscal year ends, and the books are closed. Subsequently, an annual audit takes place, and the annual report is prepared, a process that often involves internal and external public relations experts, photographers, consulting firms, accountants, and a team of lawyers. The whole process usually takes three months or more. So if the books are closed on December 31, the annual report should not be expected until at least March 31. A lot can happen in those three months, which explains why footnotes for subsequent events are so important.

There is no requirement that a company have such a footnote; for example, neither IBM nor Altria included a subsequent events footnote in its annual report for 2004. GM's 2004 annual report does have such a footnote; it explains a purchase of shares completed after the close of the year; a settlement negotiation with Fiat that concluded after the 2004 fiscal year-end; a layoff of 3,000 employees in the company's Lansing, Michigan, plants; and planned discontinuation of production of the Chevrolet Classic and Pontiac Grand Am models. Most people would agree that these post-year-end events are significant and would change an investor's impressions from what they would be based on the annual report without this information (and the impact of these changes financially).

Kodak's 2004 annual report also included a footnote disclosing subsequent events. These included an announcement that the company would acquire ownership in an overseas company and would be acquiring another operation. The footnote includes the financial impact of these changes.

> **Key point:** A "subsequent event" should be defined as any change occurring after the annual report's closing date that materially affects the company's valuation or profitability.

Most footnote sections conclude with a summary of *quarterly sales and earnings*, a footnote involving unaudited results. Altria's "Quarterly Financial Data" includes charts for the current and previous years with quarterly totals of net revenues, gross profit, and net earnings, and also provides EPS, dividends declared, and each quarter's high and low market prices. IBM provides the same information in a section of the annual report following the footnotes.

Depending on the circumstances, you may find nonrecurring and specialized footnotes in a company's annual report. Because these are nonrecurring, they should be read with care and interest. If the issue discussed warrants a footnote, it might also be essential to you in determining whether or not to invest in the stock.

▲ LONG-TERM TRENDS

It is quite difficult to use the annual reports of several companies for side-by-side comparisons. This is because there is no consistent format agreed upon among companies or in the accounting and auditing industry. One problem, of course, is that some industries require specialized types of information. For example, when comparing retail organizations, it is helpful to compare the number of stores opened and closed each year, the size of each store, and overall retail square feet. Factors like geographic competition, international customer base, and acquisitions often define success in a particular industry. So given these variables, it is not reasonable to expect *all* corporations to use exactly the same formula.

Key point: Uniformity would help everyone to better understand annual reports. It is logical. Financial statements are uniform, so why shouldn't the footnotes follow the same guideline?

Even so, it would be possible and reasonable to expect uniformity in the outline and sequence of the entire annual report, allowing room for expanded discussions of key elements that are unique to a particular industry. The footnotes section could easily be made uniform in sequence, titles, and contents, with additional footnotes being provided as circumstances require.

Who would set these standards? A combination of groups, working together, could develop formats that would meet everyone's needs. Three primary groups would be:

1. *Corporate financial executives.* The internal officers of companies best understand the factors involved in reporting financial outcomes and preparing annual reports. The ideas and requirements from executives in each specific industry would be important in developing uniform standards for annual reports and footnotes.

2. *Stock exchanges.* Every exchange has listing requirements and imposes these on its member companies. The exchanges would be an excellent source for developing uniform requirements for the annual report.

3. *The accounting industry.* The uniformity of financial statements is accepted as a fact of life, even though different industries have vastly different reporting requirements. The basic format of the three financial statements is familiar. These statements were developed by the accounting industry and, because this industry under-

stands the logic and organization of reporting formats, several participants could help develop uniform standards: the regulatory and oversight board, the FASB, AICPA, and numerous auditing firms.

The uniformity should involve the precise titles of footnotes, their exact sequence, and, where possible, the design and format of charts. For example, a uniform sequence could consist of the sections shown in Figure 5.1.

The number of years of information to be reported should also be specified. In footnotes as well as other sections of the annual report, some companies provide only two years of comparative data; this is appropriate in some situations, but not in all. Sections like segment information usually provide information for three years, but there is no consistency among companies as to what specifically is included, nor the number of years.

With uniformity, it would be possible to make side-by-side comparisons based on important footnote information. You would know exactly where to look in each and every annual report. And companies would be able to conform their reporting to a policy of transparency and full disclosure.

You may anticipate one argument from the accounting industry and even from corporate management: If you provide a footnote, that implies that there is something requiring special explanation. Thus, the idea that "if you include it, there must be a problem" is a possible stumbling block in the suggestion that footnotes be made uniform. But this argument lacks merit. Most people reading annual reports would benefit from knowing that the format, titles, and types of information provided in each section will be comparable from one organization to the next.

This type of change—like most major changes in the complex business environment—will take time and coordinated effort on many fronts. However, from the nonaccountant investor's point of view, the current reporting formats are frustrating and difficult. The fact that many web sites are difficult to navigate, use different methods for linking to annual reports, and often don't include the entire annual report online makes your job even more difficult.

In Chapter 6, you will find useful methods for uncovering the most important types of information reported in footnotes.

FIGURE 5.1

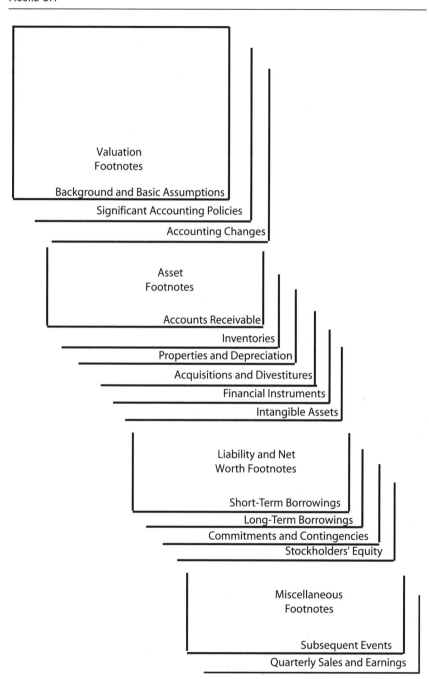

Valuation
Footnotes

Background and Basic Assumptions
Significant Accounting Policies
Accounting Changes

Asset
Footnotes

Accounts Receivable
Inventories
Properties and Depreciation
Acquisitions and Divestitures
Financial Instruments
Intangible Assets

Liability and Net
Worth Footnotes

Short-Term Borrowings
Long-Term Borrowings
Commitments and Contingencies
Stockholders' Equity

Miscellaneous
Footnotes

Subsequent Events
Quarterly Sales and Earnings

CHAPTER 6

FOOTNOTES, PART 2

RED FLAGS YOU CAN FIND ON YOUR OWN

The footnotes are disclosures of important information. They expand upon the mere numbers shown in the financial statements and explain what goes into those numbers, how valuation is set, and what circumstances may affect future profits and valuation. But there is more.

Properly used, footnotes also provide clear warning signs that things are going wrong. If you know what to look for in the footnotes, you can identify the most likely problems in three key areas: cash flow, capitalization, and operations (revenues, expenses, and earnings).

▲ ESSENTIAL RATIOS AS SOURCES OF RED FLAGS

If you know what to look for, you can find the red flags that let you know that a company is in financial trouble, or that the numbers are not behaving the way a reasonable analyst would expect them to. To most nonaccountants, financial analysis is complex, mysterious, and elusive. However, it does not have to be. In Chapter 3, you found a list of seven essential ratios, broken down into three categories:

1. Working capital.

The *current ratio* compares current assets and liabilities.

The *quick assets ratio* is similar to the current ratio, but without inventory.

Inventory turnover compares inventory and direct costs.

2. Capitalization.

The *debt ratio* shows the sources from which operations are funded.

3. Profitability.

Gross margin compares gross profit to revenues.

Expense level is a study of expenses as a percentage of revenues.

Net return compares earnings to revenues.

These seven ratios hold the key to effective analysis, for two reasons. First, they define financial health and growth potential. Second, they are the most likely sources for locating the most revealing red flags on annual reports. The footnotes are the source of supplemental information that will either (1) explain away an apparent inconsistency in these ratios or (2) provide additional information confirming the problem.

Key point: The seven essential ratios are the key to effective analysis. They define financial health and growth potential, and they point out the red flags.

Here is a suggested approach to simplified analysis of a company based on its annual report:

1. *Study the financial statements and track the seven key ratios.* Start by looking over the company's current financial statements. Apply the seven key ratios to begin to develop a picture of the company's trends, current valuation and profitability, and consistency from year to year in the financial summaries.

2. *Take the study back three years or more and establish a trend.* A study of financial ratios cannot be limited to a single year; you need to track these ratios over at least three years to determine the

trend. In some ratios, a *trend* is defined as a change from one period to the next—hopefully a strengthening trend, such as growth in revenues. Other trends involve consistency and low volatility. For example, a current ratio or debt ratio that remains at a similar percentage level each year establishes a reassuring trend of consistency.

3. *Look for departures from the trend.* Whenever there is a change in an established trend, you need to look into the reason for it. If the change is negative—such as a drastic reduction in earnings after many years of steady growth—there should be a complete explanation. It may be that a nonrecurring event caused the aberration, meaning that no real or permanent change has occurred. Or it may be that financial and market conditions have changed for the company.

4. *Seek answers or confirmation in the footnotes.* The answers can invariably be found in the footnotes. When trends change, there are always explanations. In this chapter, some specific, common examples of changes in trends are provided, along with explanations of how to interpret them. The negative changes are emphasized because, invariably, these are the types of trend movements that you need to be aware of in order to make informed investment decisions (selling stock that you already own or deciding not to buy).

Limiting your analysis to these seven key ratios may be comforting and may help you to avoid getting bogged down in a struggle with complex financial statistics. These seven ratios are at the very least a starting point for a more detailed analysis. They are not always going to provide the whole story; in some cases, you need to study details beyond the common ratios to better understand what is going on.

Key point: Limit your initial investigation to the seven basic ratios to avoid making the process overly complex or overwhelming.

For example, a study of results for Wal-Mart and Sears between 1999 and 2003 revealed a puzzling trend: Sears's revenues and earnings were falling in its retail segment, while Wal-Mart's numbers continued to rise steadily each year. The ratios alone did not explain *why* this was happening, and it often occurs in analysis that the numbers themselves show only conclusions and don't provide the underlying reasons for a trend. In the case of Sears and Wal-Mart, a close study of key financial information revealed that Wal-Mart was adding stores and retail space each year, while Sears was closing stores and losing retail space. The underlying *cause* of the trend was apparently a weakness in Sears's ability to compete, defined by an expectation that retail space *should* grow each year. In comparison, Wal-Mart established a very successful competitive trend.

A trend contains the conclusions, which is where most analysis starts and stops. But it is often more interesting to find the underlying causes for a trend. These causes provide the important insight that every investor needs. In the comparison between Wal-Mart and Sears, for example, the information discovered in investigating the cause of the revenue trend was explained by the study of stores and retail space. An investor who is interested in finding a long-term retail investment needs this type of information. It is not enough to simply compare the financial trends and pick the company with the best ratios; the effect is essential, of course, but the cause is equally important.

The answers to questions raised by trends are invariably discovered in the footnotes. In some cases, you need to check other sections of the annual report as well. For example, the store analysis and retail space trends for Wal-Mart and Sears were located in the key financial summary sections, which were not part of the footnotes. But these data, supplemented with the segment information footnotes, told the whole story, including both the effect *and* the cause.

▲ Complexity as a Warning Sign

Hindsight is always helpful, but it is not available when you are trying to decide which stock to buy. The best-known example is Enron Corporation, whose annual reports were complex because they involved a labyrinth of as many as 3,000 off-balance-sheet partnerships and subsidiaries, questionable accounting decisions, and big-number adjustments. It took everyone by surprise when Enron admitted its accounting problems in 2001.

One of the troubling aspects of the Enron situation was that the numbers were intentionally made complex. Unfortunately, most analysts gave up on trying to interpret these complexities and simply accepted Enron as what it appeared to be: a powerhouse company whose stock would continue rising endlessly.

Key point: If the explanations are too complex, that in itself could be a red flag. Even the experts can be fooled—and have been—by complicated arguments.

When corporate officers actually conspire to hide the facts and to fool everyone—investors, analysts, regulators, the Dow Jones Company, mutual funds—discerning those facts with normal ratio analysis may be impossible. If the level of fraud and deception is such that the experts are fooled, there remains only one solution: If the explanations make no sense and you cannot get straight answers, stay away from the stock. Some mutual fund managers could not decipher Enron's footnotes, so they made inquiries at the company. They were unable to get clarification, so they did not invest in the stock. Unfortunately, most fund managers, including managers at some of the largest mutual fund companies, were not able to recognize Enron's problems. But anyone can make the judgment that explanations are unclear. Footnotes *should* explain circumstances so that everyone can make sense out of the conditions that exist. A large volume of off-balance-sheet partnerships and subsidiaries is itself a huge red flag, as everyone now recognizes.

The problems of Enron, WorldCom, Tyco, and other corporations that were in the news in the 2001–2002 period have been responded to, in some ways, with the passage of new federal laws, new listing requirements by the stock exchanges, and the creation of a public accounting oversight board. The last is intended to ensure that auditing companies do not get too close to the companies they are supposed to audit, and that the auditing team remains objective and fair in its opinions.

Complexity in a footnote can be managed in one of several ways:

1. *Call the stockholder relations department.* A telephone call or e-mail to the company is a wise first step. Ask questions about any footnote that does not make sense to you, and expect clear answers. If you cannot get clarification, it could be a red flag telling you that there is a potential problem with the financial statements, some issue that the company does not want to reveal.

2. *Research the issue.* Use the Internet to find out what a specific footnote means and how it affects a company's value. If you subscribe to a brokerage company or research service, ask your questions there. If your service does not know the answer, that is another red flag, both for the company and for the service on which you depend.

3. *Check with your broker or adviser.* Your professional adviser, whom you pay for expert advice, should be able to explain any footnote to you. In fact, you will find out how professional your adviser is when you ask specific questions about footnotes and fundamental analysis. Advisers *should* be well versed in these issues, although many are not. If your adviser cannot answer your question or tries to tell you that the issue is not important, you may need to seek more qualified help.

4. *Talk to other investors.* Mastering the complexities of the footnotes is a daunting task. This is why investors are wise to team together. If you belong to an investment club or are a member of an investors' association, you may find valuable resources within your own group. Investment clubs have historically performed well because fundamental research is shared among many individual members and supplemented with a professional adviser's help. Investment associations (such as the American Association of Individual Investors, or AAII, at www.aaii.com) also provide information and assistance to members.

Key point: Accounting is complex, but effective communication, designed with transparency in mind, can work to simplify explanations and make annual reports more accessible.

The common belief that accounting is too complex for nonaccountants to understand conflicts with the objective of transparency. Many corporations "talk the talk" when it comes to communicating with stockholders and providing insights into how their financial statements are put together. The real test, however, is how well the footnotes are explained. Given that some legalese is a necessary attribute of footnotes, it remains possible for companies to attempt to clarify the material points for their nonaccountant investors and would-be investors.

▲ SEEKING THE SIMPLE EXPLANATION

Some apparently negative signals can be explained logically and reasonably. For example, a company may show a drastic fall in overall profits from one year to the next. Altria, for example, showed the following results for 2002 and 2003:[1]

(IN MILLIONS)		
	2003	2002
NET REVENUES	$81,320	$79,933
OPERATING EARNINGS	14,609	17,945

At first glance, it looks as if Altria's revenues rose while its earnings fell. This could be a red flag, but in fact, the numbers make sense when all of the facts are studied. In the segment reporting section of the footnotes, two important factors come to light:

First, in 2002, Altria sold its Miller Beer segment, so net revenues and earnings for that year include $2.641 billion from the sale. Adjusting the numbers with the beer segment sale in mind, Altria had the following core results:

(IN MILLIONS)		
	2003	2002
NET REVENUES	$81,320	$77,292
OPERATING EARNINGS	14,609	15,304

Second, Altria began an ongoing reduction in domestic tobacco sales as part of its involvement in federal and state litigation and a widespread recognition of the health problems associated with smoking. The domestic tobacco segment reported revenue for the two years of:

(IN MILLIONS)		
	2003	2002
DOMESTIC TOBACCO	$17,001	$18,877

This comparison and analysis explains the reduction in both revenue and earnings. The combination of the sale of Miller Beer and reduced domestic tobacco sales makes the point that Altria's numbers—with revenues growing while earnings fell—are quite reasonable. In fact, an analysis of the segments shows strong growth for the company, especially in its food divisions.

It would make no sense to attempt to find a complex reason for the trend when the simple explanation makes sense. As a guiding principle, it saves time and effort to start an analysis by looking for the obvious, simple reasons for a trend. In this case, a quick study of the segment information footnote explains the trend completely. Only after eliminating the obvious should your analysis move beyond it to more complex study.

As complicated as footnotes can become, the obvious, simple answers to any questions that come up are usually sufficient. However, your interest in finding red flags extends to those situations beyond the obvious. In the following sections, you will find explanations and examples of the types of problems you are likely to encounter when companies have weakening results or when companies avoid reporting their numbers because something has gone wrong. Under the Sarbanes-Oxley Act of 2002, for example, a company's CEO and CFO are required to certify the company's financial statements. A false certification can lead to both civil and criminal penalties, so this is a serious requirement. If you read that the officers have failed to certify the results or that they have missed filing deadlines, those are huge red flags.

Key point: The new law requires executives to stand behind their financial statements. Penalties for fraud are severe. This doesn't mean that fraud will never occur, only that it can be punished at a more serious level.

Some investors have bought shares in companies even when red flags were clearly visible. Among the reasons for these ill-advised decisions are:

1. *Lack of knowledge about the existence of the red flag.* The most common problem investors experience when they buy stock in the wrong company is that they did not look for red flags. They may not have known where to look for them or even that such warnings signs existed.

2. *Failure to appreciate the importance of the red flag.* Some investors read the news of problems such as failure to meet filing deadlines and, without investigating further, buy stock anyhow (or continue holding stock when they might have been better off selling it right away).

3. *Wishful thinking and misplaced loyalty to the company.* Some investors buy and hold stock for the wrong reasons. For example, should you buy shares in Krispy Kreme because you like its doughnuts? Its stock fell from a high of over $40 to $6 per share as of the end of 2005, but does that matter? Also in late 2005, the company announced that it was going to miss its deadline for filing financial statements with the SEC. The company also asked its lenders for an extension of time to repay its debt. These red flags, taken collectively, spelled trouble for the company. And the warning signs were obvious. If nothing else, a lack of information resulting from a company's inability to meet its filing deadline implies that something is very wrong.

Just as apparently bad news may have a logical and obvious explanation (such as Altria's revenue and earnings trends), the same can be true of apparently good news. Apparent negative information may hide a trend that is actually positive, but apparent positive information may actually hide bad news. When you find such a situation, a logical interpretation can save you from an expensive decision. The footnotes are the place to begin the search for red flags.

▲ CASH FLOW RED FLAGS

Cash flow is the first of the three major areas of the financial statements that are worthy of study. Footnotes may (or may not) explain the underlying causes for seemingly weak cash flow trends. If you study a three-year period, you should be able to draw meaningful conclusions about the strength or weakness of a company's cash flow.

For example, Papa John's International, Inc. (PZZA) reported a current ratio of 0.8 for all three years between 2002 and 2004. This is a very weak current ratio, given that the general standard for an acceptable current ratio is 2 to 1 or better. As a franchise pizza organization, Papa John's should not be expected to have to carry large inventories, so its relatively poor current ratio is the first indication of possible weakness in cash flow. But because the current ratio remains unchanged, an initial possibility is that the problem is not getting worse.

Upon further examination, though, the numbers reveal a growing *problem* with cash flow. You can study certain types of data in the footnotes and on the financial statements to draw this conclusion. A summary:

	2004	2003	2002
CASH FLOW PER SHARE	$ 3.12	$ 3.61	$ 3.87
CURRENT ASSETS ($000)	89.1	62.5	57.4
LONG-TERM DEBT ($000)	78.5	61.0	140.0
REVENUES ($000)	942	917	946
OPERATING INCOME ($000)	73.4	99	123

When each of these trends is studied alone, it is not especially revealing, but when they are put together, a troubling cash flow picture emerges. Cash flow per share fell each year. This makes no sense given the consistent 0.8 to 1 current ratio (meaning that current assets were *less* than current liabilities). Since the current ratio remained unchanged over three years, why was the cash flow per share on the decline?

The answer is found in a comparison between current assets and long-term debt. Note that total current assets *rose* each year, even though operating income fell. How was this possible? The answer: Long-term debt increased from 2003 to 2004, and the proceeds bolstered the current ratio to make it appear level. If you consider the volatility in long-term debt, the cash flow problem becomes apparent. Operating income fell each year, so it made no sense that the current ratio did not reflect this decline—until you looked at the long-term debt for the same period.

An examination of the footnote "Debt and Credit Arrangements" (located at www.papajohns.com) reveals the existence of a line of credit, its terms, its expiration date, and other details, but it provides no insight into how the line of credit was used by the company over the three-year period. No light was shed on the company's use of long-term debt. It appears that the maintenance of the current ratio during a period of falling profits was achieved through the line of credit.

> **Key point:** Some companies use debt to maintain the *appearance* of consistent health in their working capital. Such manipulation is troubling because it is a deceptive practice.

Is this a red flag? Any long-term investor would have to be concerned about weak cash flow in a food operation. In order to expand franchise operations aggressively and then support them, cash flow is an integral requirement. Over the long term (10 years), revenues rose steadily, and the only decline was in 2003. Operating income was less promising, however. It rose dramatically from 1999 through 2002, but fell off in the following two years. Cash flow per share followed this "wave" (rising and falling) effect. Because the latest entries in the cash flow trend were negative, it is questionable whether the company can sustain a long-term growth plan. The current ratio also weakened over the 10-year period. In 1995, it stood at 2.3 to 1, then declined until 1998, when it was 1.6 to 1—still positive, but not as strong as in previous years. The further decline to the 2004 level of 0.8 to 1 was troubling. Current liabilities rose during the entire 10-year period, outpacing the corresponding rise in current assets and causing the decline in the current ratio.

This was a red flag that was not addressed in any of the footnotes to the company's financial statements. In "Management's Discussion and Analysis of Financial Condition and Results of Operations," weakening earnings were explained as being due to a "competitive sales environment, operating margin pressures due to increased wages, insurance and other costs and the overall economic environment."

The decrease in cash flow was discussed in this section and was attributed partially to consolidation of a subsidiary, BIBP. Additionally, the explanation continues, "the remaining decrease is primarily due to unfavorable working capital changes, including increased levels of prepaid insurance due to the timing of payments and general premium increases, increased accounts receivable due to an extension of the timing of collections of certain items . . . and increased inventory levels."[2]

This explanation does not make complete sense. Cash flow is the same as "working capital," but the explanation is that the cash flow decrease was caused by "unfavorable working capital changes." The remaining explanation does not explain the trend itself, or why the company's ratios have diminished over time. It also does not address the "flat line" 0.8 to 1 current ratio during this period of falling profits.

▲ CAPITALIZATION RED FLAGS

The second area worthy of ratio testing, capitalization, can reveal problems with working capital and the long-term conflict between dividends (for stockholders) and interest expense (for lenders). The higher the debt ratio, the more future earnings have to be used to pay interest, and the less remains for funding expansion and for paying dividends. So the most obvious reason for tracking the debt ratio involves the management of the conflicting interests of equity and debt.

> **Key point:** The study of capitalization is not complicated. It comes down to one question: Who gets future payments, bondholders (interest) or stockholders (dividends)?

A second reason to track the debt ratio involves its misuse as a means of artificially bolstering the current ratio. An analyst might assume that this was part of the problem at Papa John's, as discussed in the previous section. But the expansion of long-term debt to create the appearance of working capital strength is not unusual.

In the case of Marsh & McLennan (MMC), the current ratio appears to have been steady at about 1 to 1 each year. In fact, this consistency extends back 10 full years, with only a small variance during the whole decade (down as low as 0.8 to 1 and never higher than 1.1 to 1). A first impression of this current ratio is that it has been surprisingly low. Considering that the company is in the financial services business (primarily insurance brokerage as well as financial services and human resources consulting), you would expect to see a far stronger current ratio. The company should require virtually no inventory, and, since it is involved in providing services rather than products, its cash flow should be much stronger.

Second, the debt ratio rose steadily over the three years from 2002 to 2004. In 2002, the debt ratio was only 36.6 percent. It fell slightly in 2003, but by the end of 2004, it was at 48.1 percent. This substantial increase in long-term debt accounts for the consistency in the current ratio, but it burdens the company with long-term debt service and interest expense. According to the annual report (at www.mmc.com), and, specifically, 2004's Note 10 ("Debt"), the increase in long-term debt was caused mainly by a new $1.3 billion term loan booked in 2004. It is interesting to observe that cash balances increased by about one-half the amount of the new loan in the same year, the effect of which was to maintain the current ratio at a 1 to 1 level, consistent with past years.[3]

A similar problem is observed in a review of the annual report for Motorola (MOT). At first glance, the current ratio appears quite strong. Although most trends can be identified in a three-year summary, in this case we use five years because the trend developed over a longer period of time. The five-year review demonstrates the trend:

	2004	2003	2002	2001	2000
CURRENT RATIO	2.0	1.9	1.7	1.8	1.2
DEBT RATIO	25.6%	36.1%	40.6%	39.3%	19.2%
LONG-TERM DEBT ($000)	$ 4,578	$7,161	$7,674	$8,857	$4,778
CASH ($000)	$10,556	$7,877	$6,507	$6,082	$3,301

If you reviewed *only* the current ratio, you would be reassured by the fact that working capital has increased over many years. But when you expand the analysis to include the debt ratio, you discover that historical levels (about the 19.2 percent seen for 2000) suddenly began to rise in 2001. In fact, as long-term debt levels rose, so did the year-end cash balance. If long-term debt had remained at about 19 percent during this period, it is likely that the current ratio would have declined. The annual report (at www.mot.com) provides detailed explanations of the type of debt, redemption dates, and interest rates. But management's strategy is not explained in footnotes or in management's discussion. Because of this, an analyst is left to draw conclusions based on how the numbers behaved during the periods under review. Improvements in the two most recent years resulted from the company's reporting a profit after three years' net losses.

Key point: When you track the debt ratio *and* also watch the relationship between long-term debt and cash, you can often get the real picture—especially when the current ratio remains the same during periods of net losses.

The puzzling trade-off between long-term debt and cash balances led to the consistent outcome of the current ratio. But this is misleading, and cannot be considered alone. You need to make such an analysis in three steps: First, collect and study the ratios and numerical results to try to spot the *real* trend, not just the current ratio. Second, look through the annual report's footnotes and the management's discussion section to find explanations. Third, if explanations are not provided, draw your conclusions based on what the numbers and ratios reveal.

▲ REVENUE AND EARNINGS RED FLAGS

You cannot expect management to highlight any negative news. It should provide straightforward explanations, but most corporations treat the annual report as a public relations spin on a regulatory requirement. So the explanations may be absent or spun in a positive light, even when the news is bad.

One of the more serious forms of bad news is when revenue increases but profits remain the same or, worse yet, fall. What causes this? You expect to see higher earnings associated with higher revenues because, in theory at least, expenses do not change just because revenues grow. Direct costs move up and down with revenues, but expenses, while they may change somewhat, should reflect an accelerating return. Thus, a 10 percent increase in revenues should *not* be accompanied by a 10 percent increase in expenses.

When you see increases in expense levels that outpace increasing revenues, this is a serious red flag. It could have any number of causes. You will want to ensure that management is not pirating profits and giving its members large bonuses and other incentive-based pay. There should be a trade-off between nicely rewarded management results and improved financial strength for stockholders. If the situation just gets worse as revenues increase, it signals the need for caution and further investigation.

In Marsh & McLennan's annual report, no explanation was given for an alarming trend in the revenues and operating profits for the three years from 2002 to 2004. Those results showed:

	(IN $ MILLIONS)		
	2004	2003	2002
REVENUES	$12,159	$11,588	$10,440
OPERATING INCOME	$ 2,073	$ 2,887	$ 2,633

Revenues grew each year, so, naturally, reasonable people would expect to see some of those additional revenues end up at the bottom line. Instead, operating income fell in 2004. In fact, this is a reversal of a previously established trend in revenues and earnings going back a full decade, as summarized in Figure 6.1.

When viewed over an entire decade, the relative trends in revenues and earnings can be interpreted in various ways. The three-year study appears to conclude that revenues are rising, but profits are on the decline. However, the 10-year study shows a single year of decline in profits, meaning that it is not clear whether a new trend has been established and an old one reversed.

You will recall from a previous analysis that the company's debt ratio was rising during this period, with a consistent current ratio level of about 1 to 1. Collectively, these weak signals should concern an analyst. Even if the revenue/profits trend is unclear, what about the other signals? Why

FIGURE 6.1

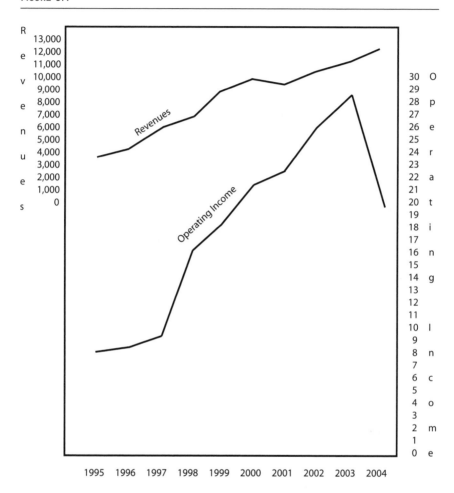

Source: S&P Stock Report, Lucent Technologies, December 2005.

did profits fall in 2004? Why was the current ratio unchanged, and what is the connection with the rising debt ratio?

Key point: If revenues are up but profits are flat or declining, the reason should be determined. This is one of the key negative indicators that is worth looking for and questioning.

The same questions could be asked regarding the operating results reported by the McKesson Corporation (MCK). The results for the three years ending in fiscal 2005 (March 31 year-end) showed the following:

	(IN $ MILLIONS)		
	2005	2004	2003
REVENUES	$80,515	$69,506	$57,121
OPERATING INCOME	$ 1,260	$ 1,216	$ 1,134

These results raise questions. Revenues increased dramatically, but operating income remained flat. However, in the company's fiscal 2005 annual report (at www.mckesson.com), a very complete and detailed explanation was provided. In the management's discussion and analysis section, a lower gross margin was explained as "declines in sales margin due to a shift in customer mix and competitive pressures." This is the type of explanation you see a lot in management's discussions when the outcomes were negative. It really means, "The customer mix changed, and our competitors hurt our bottom line."

The discussion goes on to provide more meaningful explanations, including customer settlement costs, securities litigation ($1.2 billion in fiscal 2005), and restructuring charges. While these are negative factors for the company, the explanations make sense. The strong historical revenue growth exhibited by McKesson is a promising sign for future growth, even though current litigation and restructuring charges kept recent profitability flat. Another signal of fundamental strength is the consistent current ratio, which averaged 1.4 to 1 over the past five years. During the same five-year period, the debt ratio declined from 26.1 percent to 18.6 percent.

▲ OTHER PLACES TO LOOK

The three areas worthy of study—cash flow, capitalization, and revenues/earnings—are going to be conclusive for answering many of the questions you will have in studying the annual report. But there are other, more subtle signals that could spell trouble in the future, or could indicate situations in which companies are adjusting the numbers to create a pre-determined outcome.

When companies reduce the balance of their intangible assets, it raises questions. Some companies have cited FASB opinions and rulings. These Statements of Financial Accounting Standards provide guidance for companies in their treatment of transactions. However, these statements often allow companies to change outcomes. In hindsight, in is obvious that this was what WorldCom accomplished by citing *SFAS 142* when it adjusted earnings from 1999 through 2001. The SEC investigated the matter after WorldCom filed the largest-ever bankruptcy in 2002, with estimated losses of $107 billion. The goodwill decision was not the only problem, but it was used to obscure the truth about WorldCom's financial condition. So when large adjustments and restatements of intangible assets occur, they deserve a closer look.

Another red flag, sometimes found in the footnotes as a disclosure and sometimes announced elsewhere in the annual report, is a change in auditing firms. This decision will also be reported in the financial news when the announcement is made. In the past, the reason for changing auditing firms has often been a difference of opinion about what the company can and cannot do in its accounting. A firm may resign because its client will not agree to a decision that the auditing team has made.

You will recall that *restructuring* is another word for "cutting back." Companies don't like to admit that they are downsizing in terms of facilities or employees, but when they cannot compete at their current levels, they have to incur some "restructuring costs." This is a signal that a company's future growth is doubtful and that it may be time to look at competitors within the same industry. Which competitors are expanding while the company in question is cutting employees and paying severance packages or closing manufacturing plants? A good example is Kodak, whose restructuring has been comprehensive and widespread, and whose restructuring costs stretched over several years—an indication that the company underwent a massive cutback in its overall size. Compared to the case of McKesson, where restructuring improved profitability, Kodak's endless restructuring seems to be accompanied by ever-weaker annual results.

Key point: Some words and phrases are meant to soften the impact of what is really going on. Thus, "restructuring" often means plant closures and layoffs, and "consolidation" could mean "we expanded too quickly and lost a bundle."

An especially troubling signal is high volatility in the reported revenues and earnings. Everyone likes to have some degree of predictability. You would like to see a record of steadily growing revenues and earnings without sudden and unexplained drops in those levels. In fact, you will find that when the financial numbers are predictable, the market share price tends to also be less volatile.

Consider the case of Lucent Technologies. It would be very difficult for anyone to predict the long-term trend of revenues and profits for this telecommunications equipment and software company. Whether you study three years or a full decade, the results were very volatile. For its fiscal years ending September 30, results showed the following:

(IN MILLIONS)[4]

	REVENUES	OPERATING INCOME
2004	$ 9,045	$ 1,906
2003	8,470	633
2002	12,321	(3,257)
2001	21,294	(6,336)
2000	33,813	6,308
1999	38,303	7,494
1998	30,147	3,795
1997	26,360	3,081
1996	15,859	1,424

This level of volatility—with more recent years appearing especially unsure—is a troubling sign. Not only did revenues fall, but profits followed suit. A related problem occurs with yet another red flag, large core earnings adjustments. Lucent's core earnings included substantial adjustments in 2001, 2002, and 2003—in the *billions* of dollars. Since S&P has tracked core earnings only since 2001, the following analysis includes only four years:

(IN MILLIONS)[5]

	REVENUES	OPERATING INCOME	CORE EARNINGS
2004	$ 9,045	$ 1,906	$ 754
2003	8,470	633	(1,980)
2002	12,321	(3,257)	(16,627)
2001	21,294	(6,336)	(13,160)

Lucent's adjustments were especially large, indicating serious accounting problems. In fact, stockholders in Lucent lost over a quarter trillion dollars from 1999 to 2001, with the stock going from a high of about $75 per share down to less than $10 by June 2001. Among the company's questionable practices in the 1999–2001 period were booking revenues too early, lowering its liabilities by changing its accounting methods, failing to take losses for impaired assets (assets whose actual value was lower than book value), increasing reported income in one year by reporting pension gains (a nonrecurring gain that was 16 percent of total reported income that year), creating artificial profits through treatment of reserves from 10 acquisitions, and shifting expenses to a later period by capitalizing internal software expenses.

Key point: A destructive aspect of cooking the books, beyond the obvious false report in the single year, is that it prevents you from spotting a dependable trend. Even future year is suspect as well because of the gimmicks used in the past.

That is a lot of adjusting. Lucent's practices were exceptional in two ways. First, the company engaged in numerous different deceptive practices, and second, the numbers were huge. The results, of course, show up in the historical comparison between revenues and profits, and even more so in the company's core earnings.

Logically, when a company files for bankruptcy, the stock price invariably declines. As a red flag, bankruptcy is obvious; however, if you watch the financial trends over time, you can probably see it coming. For example, Boyd's Bears (BOYD) was a popular manufacturer of collectibles for many years. However, within a few short years after the company went public, its revenues and profits came in at ever-lower numbers each year. In October 2005, the company filed for Chapter 11 bankruptcy. In the year 2005 alone, the stock value went from more than $5 per share down to 4 cents by year-end. The most important lesson in this is not that the company failed, but that anyone looking through the financial statements could see it coming.

Finally, an important warning signal that does not always show up anywhere in the annual report (but that can be found by following the financial news) is a missed regulatory filing deadline. Every listed company is required to make periodic financial reports to the SEC, and when a deadline is missed, it usually means that there is a big problem. For example, the popular doughnut franchise Krispy Kreme (KKD) reported in late 2005 that it would miss its third-quarter filing deadline for its SEC report. Even more alarming, the company had not filed financial statements with the SEC for over a year. Management denied rumors that the company was heading for bankruptcy; but when companies miss their filing deadlines, the question of solvency invariably comes up, and for good reason.[6]

Looking for red flags in the footnotes is not difficult. With the help of a reliable reporting service such as the S&P Stock Reports, you can find enough reliable information to interpret the numbers accurately. You do not need an accounting degree, just an understanding of the short list of important ratios worth tracking. In the next chapter, other sections of the annual report are studied in their dual context: disclosure information required by law and public relations messages used by the corporation to encourage investors to buy and hold stock.

CHAPTER 7

STRUCTURE OF THE ANNUAL REPORT

A PUBLIC RELATIONS DOCUMENT

The annual report can be a confusing document because it serves so many different purposes. Its various "audiences" are not always coordinated, and the purpose of each may conflict with the others. The three major reasons the annual report is prepared are:

1. *Public relations.* The corporate point of view is that the annual report is an opportunity to trumpet the corporation's achievements, its success, and its markets. Many pages—usually near the front of the report—are dedicated to a discussion of markets and marketing programs. It is rare for a company to admit in this section that it did not compete well in its sector (although other sections may cite "competitive factors" as a reason for declining sales and profits). As an orientation to the markets that the company serves, this is a useful section, but it is wise to look at the information with its emphasis on the positive in mind, and to recognize that it is not the whole story. Some investors read *only* this section of the report. Admittedly, it is far more interesting than the financial statements and footnotes, and usually includes colorful charts and dazzling photos, but the public relations efforts put forth in the annual report do not always tell the whole story.

2. *Regulatory.* Companies are required to publish audited financial statements. These are filed with the SEC and are also required by state regulatory agencies. They must be made available to the public, and virtually all listed companies include links on their web sites to an "investors" section, where complete annual reports are available. But the regulatory sections are mixed in with the glossy photos and charts of the public relations portions of the annual report.

3. *Investor information.* Beyond the regulatory requirement that companies publish financial information, investors want to know about their companies on several levels. They are interested in the markets in which the company is involved, and they make judgments about its effectiveness in a competitive environment. The annual report also includes information about quarterly revenue and earnings, stock price high and low numbers, earnings per share, and dividends. The "selected financial data" section provides highlights for a number of years. Most annual reports list three or five years' results, while others include information for up to 10 years. A desirable transparency is realized to a degree in the sections of the annual report aimed at investors, but *real* and *complete* transparency is a work in progress and may take many years to achieve.

▲ THE PREMISES OF THE ANNUAL REPORT

The combined public relations, regulatory, and investor information in the annual report needs to be reviewed with several factors in mind. No single factor can allow you to make a decision about whether to buy the company's stock or, if you already own it, whether to keep it in your portfolio. You need to look at a range of factors, and this is where the three different purposes of the annual report are valuable when looked at together. These matters include:

1. *The financial strength of the company and its operating results.* The first point of interest is invariably going to involve some very fundamental questions: Is the company well capitalized? How much of its capitalization is equity and how much is debt? Is there a trend changing this mix underway? Are revenues and earnings growing, flat, or shrinking? Is the company even profitable? What kinds of core earnings adjustments

are being noted by S&P? You may be able to eliminate many candidates by going through a short list of fundamental questions and applying financial ratios. As noted in previous chapters, these ratios need to be reviewed collectively and not individually in order to spot actual trends and to see through any manipulation of the numbers.

2. *Levels of volatility.* Most investors and analysts agree that *price volatility* is a sound test of market risk, or at least one test among many. As a technical indicator, price volatility is a valuable test, especially when applied in combination with fundamental tests. However, a review of a company's *fundamental volatility* is also valuable. This is a reference to the trends in revenues and earnings. Are the numbers fairly consistent and do they move in the same direction each year, or do they change drastically? A related test is that of core earnings versus reported earnings; in well-managed companies, there is a tendency for core earnings adjustments to be relatively low. You will also find that when fundamental volatility is low and core earnings adjustments are small, the price volatility tends to be low as well. The translation: Fundamentally low volatility means lower risk, whether volatility is measured by the revenue and earnings numbers or by the market price.

3. *The company's competitive position and history.* People often pick companies using illogical criteria. For example, if you use a company's product or like its type of product line, is that enough reason to buy its stock? Everything has its cycle, and, because of changes in technology, culture, and geography, some products become obsolete. The Polaroid camera and Kodak film are modern examples; digital technology has made the instant camera and old-style film expensive and impractical.

4. *News and events.* The annual report is only one of many sources of information. If you plan to invest in the market, it makes sense to pay attention to the financial news as well. Online brokerage sites provide daily headlines, for example. So if you are considering investing in a company and you have studied its financial statements, read its annual report, and tracked the stock's trading patterns, that is a good start. But why put money into a stock if the company has not filed its financial statements on time, has defaulted on repayment of loans, or has filed for bankruptcy? The financial news is a crucial source of current information that augments the annual report and the interim quarterly reports.

5. *Contingent liabilities.* Clearly, some industries and specific companies have been exposed to a higher than average number of lawsuits, or at least the possibility of lawsuits in the near future. The tobacco and pharmaceutical industries are examples. Even well-managed and well-capitalized companies like Altria and Merck have significant contingencies, and studying this aspect of the footnotes is essential. Anyone investing in companies with high contingencies should know the scope of those potential problems before buying stock.

6. *Diversification of products.* The product or mix of products offered by a company often has everything to do with its competitive position and its long-term growth prospects. A single-product company is vulnerable to diversified competition, changes in technology, and a limited marketplace. Diversification opens up new markets and is an important attribute of a well-managed company with farsighted management. Diversification as an effective management strategy is a skill that management needs to possess and apply.

> **Key point:** A study of how companies manage their long-term competitive position—upgrading for new technology, for example—is instructive, especially when an industry leader is slow to accept change.

For example, several years ago, Kodak downplayed the importance of digital technology and announced that it continued to think of film as its primary market. Several years later, the company had to scramble to catch up with its competitors as fewer people continued to use film cameras. The extensive restructuring that Kodak has undergone and the volatility of its stock price as well as its revenues and earnings is a consequence of the company's slow acceptance of change.

Another example is Altria Corporation, a major cigarette manufacturer. As cultural awareness of the health risks of smoking become more widespread, several changes occurred. The company (previously named Philip Morris) changed its name, it began reducing its emphasis on domestic tobacco sales, invested in Kraft Foods and other profitable non-tobacco subsidiaries, and it took a lead in education about the health problems of smoking. Although litigation expenses continue to represent a major contingency for Altria, it has taken positive steps to diversify into other industries.

The following sections examine other important parts of the annual report and give examples of how specific companies have communicated with regulators, analysts, and investors through each section.

▲ THE CHAIRMAN'S LETTER

Most corporations highlight the letter from the chairman and/or CEO. This "letter to stockholders" is intended as a direct message from top management, advising each and every investor of the key changes, events, and operational facts for the past year.

In practice, the letter is rarely written by the top executive. It is usually crafted by an internal or external public relations department in consultation with the company's executives. Of course, important changes have to be addressed in this letter, if only to mollify stockholders whose stock may have declined in value, or who have read in the financial news that the company is heading for insolvency. However, the purpose of the letter to stockholders is often far different from its stated purpose. The real mission of the letter is to put a positive spin on everything, even when the news is really negative.

Lucent Technologies began its 2004 "To Our Shareholders" section with this paragraph:

> Fiscal 2004 was a pivotal year for our company. For the first time since 2000, we posted a profitable year and achieved annual revenue growth. We also generated cash from operations. Further, we developed a clear vision for the next generation of communications and put in place capabilities to be our customers' partner of choice. We achieved this through our relentless focus on growth opportunities in the marketplace, solid execution and controlling our costs and expenses.[1]

The reported year was "pivotal" in the sense that the company reported revenues above those for the previous year, but this is hardly a firmly established trend: Revenues peaked in 1999 and declined each year from then until 2003; 2004 was the first year since 1999 when revenues rose. But 2004's revenues were less than one-fourth the reported revenues only five years before. In addition, investors should be aware of Lucent's serious accounting irregularities of only a few years before; these questionable practices included prebooked revenues, capitalized expenses, and many other violations.

> **Key point:** A "trend" may, in fact, be only a change of direction for a single year. Real trends need to be firmly established before they can be so labeled.

Statements in the letter to shareholders such as "we developed a clear vision for the next generation of communications" and references to "our relentless focus on growth opportunities" do not necessarily mean anything substantial. These public relations statements sound strong and positive, but what do they actually mean?

The letter goes on to highlight positive financial results for the year, but it focuses on the one-year changes and not on the trend going back three, five, or ten years, where the numbers look much worse. The letter is full of glowing statements such as "our people made the difference" and "we have weathered the storm." Given the fact that the good news is limited to one year, it could have been premature to announce victory at the end of 2004.

You may also note how companies cast news in the best possible (or least damaging) light. For 2004, when Lucent's revenues were up, the "To Our Stockholders" letter claims direct responsibility for success. In the previous year, however, when revenues had fallen from prior levels, the letter's tone was quite different, blaming the industry and the market. The 2003 letter began:

> Fiscal 2003 was another challenging year for the global telecommunications market as capital spending by service providers continued to decline before beginning to stabilize toward the end of the year. Despite market difficulties, we managed to reduce our year-over-year losses substantially and end the year on a strong positive note—reporting a profitable quarter for the first time since March

2000 and generating positive operating cash flow for the first time since June 2002.[2]

This somewhat different tone emphasizes the positive fourth quarter, a skillful example of how a very negative outcome (compared to past results) can be made to sound as positive as possible.

Another company, Kodak, experienced no real growth in revenues over the decade ending in 2004; operating income declined over the same period, and S&P core earnings (calculated only since 2001) were dismal. A summary:[3]

IN MILLIONS

YEAR	REVENUES	OPERATING INCOME	S&P CORE EARNINGS
2004	$13,517	$1,638	$(119)
2003	13,317	1,685	149
2002	12,835	2,898	127
2001	13,324	1,923	(541)
2000	13,994	3,103	
1999	14,089	2,908	
1998	13,406	2,783	
1997	14,538	2,431	
1996	15,967	3,107	
1995	14,980	2,841	

The Kodak annual report for 2004 contained very upbeat introductory paragraphs in its "Management's Letter." It began:

> In its first full year of its digital transformation strategy, Kodak came out of the gate at a full gallop—and we continue to build momentum.
>
> From robust digital revenue growth, to our ability to manage effectively the decline in our traditional film business, to fulfillment of our digital acquisitions plan, our results are evidence we are building a more diversified, leaner, stronger Kodak for the future.
>
> Simply stated: our strategy is on course.[4]

It is true that the digital segment of Kodak accounted for 64 percent of overall revenue in 2004, a sign that the company is aggressively transforming its operations. However, the ongoing restructuring programs at Kodak were significant, involving layoffs of as many as 25,000 people, according to the company's 2005 estimates. The long-term problems at Kodak, including its late entry into the digital market, were reflected in its stock price. In 1997, the price range was between $94.75 and $53.31 per share. In 2004, the range was between $34.75 and $24.25.

> **Key point:** During periods of great turmoil and change, companies are not likely to highlight their internal chaos. Rather, they will tend to emphasize the positive whenever possible, even if it is only a speck of hope in a dismal sea of bad news.

The 2004 letter cites the company's "quick response to shifting demand," but, in fact, its transition—reflected in both revenues and profits—was slow. The 2004 letter highlights some positive changes, but Kodak's long-term picture is dismal, and it remains to be seen whether the optimism of the company's CEO and its president was justified. This is an example of a company whose numbers do not support the enthusiasm expressed in the letter.

General Motors, the world's largest auto manufacturer, has serious problems involving its pension liabilities. If those liabilities were reported on its balance sheet, the company would have a *negative* net worth. The historical financial results at first appear positive; revenues and operating income grew steadily throughout the decade ending in 2004, but long-term debt in 2004 was 85.5 percent of total capitalization, compared to 61.1 percent in 1995. The chairman's letter begins:

> The cover of this 2004 General Motors Annual Report says, "Hands on the wheel. Eyes on the road." What exactly does that mean to GM? It means we're driving ahead with confidence . . . and we are well aware of the obstacles in our path. We are staying focused on designing and building the best-engineered, best-looking, highest-value cars and trucks that provide millions of people around the world the freedom of mobility. As I concluded in last year's letter to you, becoming the best is an unending journey, a constantly changing destination. We've come a long way on that trip.[5]

This very positive statement is somewhat justified when you look at the trends in revenues and operating income. However, GM's problems have not disappeared. The market price of the stock has declined over the previous decade as a result of worries about the company's capitalization, continued growth in pension liabilities, and continuing competitive factors. In 1999, the stock reached a high value of close to $95 per share, but by 2004, its market value was less than half that level, and S&P set a 12-month target price of only $21 per share, down from the $37–$56 per share range of 2004. Rumors about the company's possible bankruptcy had much to do with the weakness in the market, reflecting growing long-term debt and dismal net income (compared to operating income). The growth in long-term debt was a large factor; 2004 interest expense was nearly $12 billion, compared to only $5.4 billion a decade earlier.

So the enthusiastic and positive tone of the GM letter was not entirely justified. Like most letters found in annual reports, this letter emphasized positive results, and nothing was said about the capitalization deterioration or pension liability problems.

Another company that had problems in its financial reporting was Krispy Kreme. At the end of 2005, the company had not filed quarterly reports for more than a year, and other danger signals were present as well—the resignation of one of its directors, a new announcement that a quarterly filing deadline was going to be missed, and the news that the company had amended its credit agreements with lenders, including a six-month extension for filing financial reports. All of these ominous negative signals were accompanied by the lack of annual reports on the company web site.

The letter to shareholders is not an especially revealing document in most situations. If the news is good, it is obvious from a quick review of the numbers. If the news is bad, the only value of the letter is to appreciate how language can be used to express negative results in glowing terms. When a company talks about "reduced levels of net losses" it may mean simply that "we lost money again, but not quite as much as last year." And when the chairman's letter talks about "a reinvigorated and far-sighted approach to creating a leaner, more efficient operation," it could be another way of saying, "We are laying off thousands of workers to try to cut losses, but so far nothing seems to be working." If you do read the letter to stockholders, you often need to read *between* the lines to get the real story.

▲ MARKETS AND MARKETING PROGRAMS

Another section of the annual report that is primarily a public relations effort is the one containing those glossy photos of happy employees, clean production plants, and products stacked up in warehouses. Here, too, you run into the public relations slogans that mean nothing but sound great. GM's "Hands on the wheel, eyes on the road" is a good example; the slogan is presented over an action shot of a new car. The GM 2004 annual report contained additional slogans like "driven to excite," "bring it on," and "drive one company further." There were so many slogans— including the cliché "families first"—that the transition from the visual and public relations section to the detailed financial report that followed was jarring.

> **Key point:** If you recognize the difference between being sold something and being given hard facts, you will do well in deciphering the annual report. Hype, seen with meaningless slogans, often is used to shield the bad news.

Motorola's "Why Motorola? Why now? What's next?" and Exxon-Mobil's "Taking on the world's toughest energy challenges" are further examples of the slogan-driven promotions that you find in the introductions, cover sheets, and market sections of annual reports.

The market descriptions of annual reports are quite useful in gaining an overview of a company's diversification. For example, many people don't know that Altria (known best for its Philip Morris tobacco brands) also owns Kraft Foods; that Kodak owns Creo, Inc., a supplier of systems used in commercial printing operations; or that Marsh & McLennan (a well-known insurance and risk management corporation) owns Putnam Investments, whose mutual funds family has $213 billion under management. Getting an overview of a company's holdings and of its geographic influence is revealing. For example, a majority of Kodak's revenue is derived outside the United States, and Altria's tobacco and food operations both have strong nondomestic revenues and earnings.

The markets and marketing section of the annual report is without any doubt aimed at promoting the company. However, beyond the obvious public relations motivation on the company's part, you will gain insight by reading this section carefully, especially if you look for these four things:

1. *Specific information about the company's range of products and markets.* Investors should know the details about companies whose stock they buy. Attributes and elements of risk cannot be fully appreciated until these details are known. For example, if you were considering buying Kodak stock, it would be crucial to understand the company's competitive position in the digital technology areas of its broader market. In thinking about buying Altria stock, you would want to review the contingencies associated with ongoing tobacco litigation, and the same would apply to Merck and its contingencies related to Vioxx. The range of products and markets tells you not only about a company's exposure to risk, but also about its profit opportunities. Many years ago, Lucent was attractive because, as a former segment of AT&T, the company was a leader in the emerging telecommunications industry, especially the wireless telephone business. However, its serious accounting irregularities distorted the numbers, so that it is difficult to identify trends. More time may be required; meanwhile, it would be important to understand that Lucent does not just sell one product. It is a major player in switching, access, and optical networking products. These vital and growing industries make Lucent a potentially strong growth stock.

2. *Geographic influence and markets.* The obvious markets are rarely the whole story. Companies like Altria, Kodak, and Wal-Mart are well known in the United States but are also active through international subsidiaries. For example, Altria sells 69 percent of its tobacco products overseas, and 55 percent of its total revenues were foreign in 2004. Wal-Mart operated 1,587 stores outside the United States in 2004, nearly 44 percent of its total outlets (and providing about 20 percent of total revenue). Kodak's sales were 58 percent outside the United States. In the global economy that is emerging today, these factors are important to the long-term growth of every company. International sales represent new

markets that are essential to growth. Investors need to understand these market and competitive factors to fully appreciate the potential for future growth.

3. *Levels of diversification, especially compared to the company's competitors.* The degree of product or service diversification is an additional factor to consider. When Boyd's Bears went public with its collectible line, sales flattened and began falling. The company began acquiring competing collectible lines, which was not real diversification. Discretionary spending was finite, and acquiring competitors did not provide diversification for the company. Effective diversification, such as Altria's acquisition of Kraft Foods or Marsh & McLennan's ownership of Putnam Investments, provides the company with new markets and an expanded potential customer base. Every sector has a finite market, and diversification enables companies to identify new markets.

4. *The company's position within its industry or industries.* Is a particular company the leader in its industry? Wal-Mart is the largest retailer in the United States, and its historical record of revenues and earnings reflects its success. The stock price rose about 500 percent in the decade from 1996 to 2005. There are several ways to view competition. Buying stock in the leading company is one way to pursue continuing fundamental and market growth. But some investors prefer buying the number-two or number-three company in the industry. The theory is that holding the lead position is temporary; that position will eventually be ceded to another company. For example, Kodak, once the leader in the photographic products industry, has a much larger market cap ($6.8 billion) than Fuji Photo Film and other rivals, but its competitive position and revenue and earnings have not been impressive.

▲ MANAGEMENT'S DISCUSSION AND ANALYSIS

This section is an explanation and interpretation of the financial statements. It is usually prepared not by top management, but by accounting employees, often, with the participation of the auditing team. It is a useful section because it provides insight into management's point of view about trends and the importance of specific numbers.

Key point: It is interesting to compare the discussions provided by management with the same information presented in footnotes. If nothing else, you may gain a different point of view on the same issues.

This is the second-longest section of many annual reports, surpassed only by the footnotes. Altria's 2004 annual report requires 19 pages for its "Management's Discussion and Analysis of Financial Condition and Results of Operations." This is broken down into several subsections: "Description of the Company," "Executive Summary," "Critical Accounting Policies and Estimates," "Consolidated Operating Results," "2004 Compared with 2003," "2003 Compared with 2002," "Operating Results by Business Segment (Tobacco, Food, Beer and Financial Services)," "Financial Review," "Market Risk," "New Accounting Standards," "Contingencies," and "Cautionary Factors That May Affect Future Results."

Some of these sections mirror footnote discussions. The difference, however, is that this section is management's chance to provide explanations, whereas footnotes tend to be passive accounting interpretations and disclosures. For example, contingencies are explained in great detail in the footnotes in terms of the nature of the litigation, estimated legal costs, and historical background. But in this section, management provides more explanation, including its reasons for not setting up reserves in many instances:

ALG and its subsidiaries record provisions in the consolidated financial statements for pending litigation when they determine that an unfavorable outcome is probable and the amount of the loss can be reasonably estimated. Except as discussed in Note 19: (i) management has not concluded that it is probable that a loss has been incurred in any of the pending tobacco-related litigation; (ii) management is unable to make a meaningful estimate of the amount or range of loss that could result from an unfavorable outcome of pending tobacco-related litigation; and (iii) accordingly, management has not provided any amounts in the consolidated financial statements for unfavorable outcomes, if any.[6]

A similar level of detail can be expected from most companies. IBM's "Management Discussion" section takes up 25 pages and also contains subsections: "Road Map," "Management Discussion Snapshot," "Description of Business," "Year in Review," "Prior Year in Review," "Looking Forward," "Employees and Global Workforce," and "Global Financing."

IBM's discussion is highly detailed and complex, and, like Altria's section, it includes various comparative charts explaining its interpretation of data. The discussion section gives management a chance to give its interpretation of the financial statements, whereas the footnotes are the results of the auditing team's compilation of the same data.

▲ THE AUDITOR'S OPINION LETTER

The financial statements are prepared by an outside auditing firm, which provides an opinion letter within the annual report. As long as the auditing firm issues a "clean" opinion letter (meaning that, in its opinion, all is well), the signals are positive. But if the opinion is qualified in any way, that is a danger signal.

Given the past abuses of corporations, often approved or passively accepted by outside auditors, it is reasonable for people to remain dubious about the auditor's opinion letter. The accounting industry has not policed itself adequately (see Chapter 7), and it should be expected to have to earn the trust of the public.

Altria's 2004 opinion letter, prepared by PricewaterhouseCoopers, contains the essential statement:

> In our opinion, the accompanying consolidated balance sheets and the related consolidated statements of earnings, stockholders' equity and cash flows present fairly, in all material respects, the financial position of Altria Group, Inc. and its subsidiaries at December 31, 2004 and 2003, and the results of their operations and their cash flows for each of the three years in the period ended December 31, 2004.[7]

IBM's "Report of Independently Registered Public Accounting Firm" presents the same wording. In both of these cases, investors and analysts are assured by the outside auditing firm that it believes that the financial statements "fairly present" a true picture of the company's operations and valuation.

> **Key point:** A blessing by the auditor is always reassuring, even though recent history has shown that auditing firms are not always free from conflict of interest. This is why you need to perform your own ratio tests.

Companies do not always receive a clean opinion. For 2004, Large Scale Biology Corporation (LSBC) announced that its 2004 financial statements were issued with a *qualified* opinion. The auditing firm did not believe that the statements were fair or accurate in all respects. The specific reason cited for this was that, because of the company's negative cash flow, a "going concern qualification" was issued. This means that the auditing team raised the question of whether the company will be able to sustain itself.[8]

A company that is a going concern is assumed to have the resources to remain in business, so when an auditor's opinion is qualified by a going concern issue, that signals the possibility that the company is approaching insolvency.

Other qualified opinions can relate to actual accounting or valuation decisions. These qualifications may be limited to single transactions on which the auditors and management cannot agree (in such cases, the qualified opinion is not a blanket condemnation of the financial statements). But when the auditor refuses to issue any opinion or publishes an adverse opinion, this is a more ominous sign. If the auditors find that the company has not adhered to GAAP standards, has engaged in fraudulent practices, or lacks the proper internal procedures needed to verify the books, the auditing firm will not be able to "sign off" on the company's accounting.

▲ SELECTED FINANCIAL DATA

One of the troubling realities of annual report formatting is the inconsistency among companies. It is extremely difficult to compare selected financial data. Some companies include three years, others as many as ten; five years is most common. But some companies do not even provide multiple-year data beyond the two-year comparative financial statements.

Making the problem even more difficult, companies do not all report the same information, nor do they use the same format. For example, Altria and IBM—companies offering among the best web sites and most comprehensive annual reports—are not consistent in what data they select, although both report the data for five years. A summary of their reporting selections is shown in Table 7.1.

Although Altria's selected data are more detailed, IBM's provide the essential information regarding revenue, earnings, and valuation. It's just a matter of preference, and every corporation selects its own data; there is no coordination among companies and no established standard for what should be included.

The problem here is made more complex by the fact that some industries require specialized information. For example, in the retail sector, many corporations include summaries of the number of stores opened or closed during each year. Wal-Mart goes back ten years and breaks its numbers down by type of store, and even further by domestic and international sites.

▲ STOCKHOLDER INFORMATION AND PRICE HISTORY

Toward the end of the annual report, corporations include information specifically for stockholders, primarily involving contact information. Altria's "Shareholder Information" is the last section of its 2004 report, and it includes corporate and divisional addresses, phone numbers, and web sites; the auditors' address; a shareholder response phone number; direct stock purchase information; publications (annual reports, SEC filings); stock exchange information; and the date and location of the upcoming annual stockholders' meeting. IBM's "Stockholder Information" section contains the same basic information, but in a somewhat different format.

TABLE 7.1 SELECTED DATA COMPARISON.

Altria	IBM
"Selected Financial Data—Five-Year Review"	"Five-Year Comparison of Selected Financial Data"
Net Revenues	Income from Continuing Operations (Loss)/Income from Discontinued Operations
U.S. Export Sales	
Cost of Sales	
Federal Excise Taxes on Products	
Foreign Excise Taxes on Products	
Operating Income	
Interest and Other Debt Expense, Net	
Earnings from Continuing Operations	
Pre-Tax Profit Margin	
Provision for Income Taxes	
Cumulative Effect of Accounting Changes	
Net Earnings	Net Income
Basic Earnings per Share	Earnings per Share of Common Stock
Diluted Earnings per Share	
Dividends Declared per Share	Cash Dividends Paid on Common Stock
Weighted Average Shares (millions)	
Capital Expenditures	
Depreciation	
Property, Plant, and Equipment	Investment in Property
Inventories	
Total Assets	Total Assets
Total Long-Term Debt	Total Debt
	Working Capital
Total Deferred Income Taxes	
Stockholders' Equity	Stockholders' Equity
	Return on Stockholders' Equity
Book Value per Share Outstanding	
Market Price per Share—High/Low	
Closing Price per Share at Year-End	
Price/Earnings Ratio at Year-End	
Common Shares Outstanding, Year-End	
Number of Employees	

Key point: Providing investors with contact information is a nice touch. Unfortunately, that may be viewed as providing enough information when, in truth, corporations have a long way to go in improving the annual report.

Another section summarizes the stock price and trading range. Altria did not include this information in its annual report, and IBM's "Selected Quarterly Data" provides quarterly summaries of the operating statement and high and low stock prices. Here again, what management considers important information to disclose varies from one company to the next.

▲ THE QUEST FOR TRANSPARENCY

As this chapter has shown, a chronic problem in the reporting of financial information is that it is quite inconsistent. There is no single format. Even when corporations use similar formats, they do not include a uniform number of financial results.

The fact that public relations sections are mixed in with the purely financial and disclosure sections makes the annual report a confusing document. An even greater problem is that because the promotional sections are easier to read and are accompanied by attractive photography, it is all too easy to read only those sections, and to spend little time analyzing the financial report itself. As difficult as financial statements are for nonaccountants to read, the inconsistencies in format, sequence, and inclusion of data all make matters more confusing than they would be with a uniform reporting format.

The concept of *transparency*—that annual reports and other communications would give you the whole picture—will become reality only gradually and over many years. Today, there is very little real transparency in U.S.-based corporate annual reports. This is unfortunate.

The Sarbanes-Oxley Act of 2002 dedicated an entire section to new rules and requirements for corporate responsibility. It requires the CEO and CFO to certify their company's financial statements as accurate and complete. But there is no specific requirement that corporations make their communications transparent. In another section, "Enhanced Financial Disclosures," listed companies are required to tell investors and regulators about material adjustments proposed by auditors, off-balance-sheet transactions, pro forma financial report preparation and estimates, and management's assessment of its own internal controls. These conditions relate to compliance with technical requirements, but here again, there are no standards or guidelines for corporate transparency.

Some further reforms aimed at improving reporting methods and formats, while improving corporate transparency, should include:

1. *Further fine-tuning of the definitions of reporting standards.* Annual reports are difficult to follow because no reporting standards exist. From the corporate point of view, the design, format, and inclusion of data are all based on perceived needs, established internal practice, and specific attributes of the company's product mix, geographic markets, and accounting decisions. Sarbanes-Oxley created *requirements* for disclosure and compliance, but it did nothing to create standards for transparency. The precise data to be included in annual reports, their format, the sequence and titles of sections, and other such matters need to be formalized and made uniform.

The task of creating a uniform reporting standard for annual reports could be generated on an advisory basis by accounting firms and the GAAP establishment. But this is not a likely source of new ideas. The accounting industry has been passive and reluctant to suggest any changes, and the complexity of GAAP provides it with a great deal of flexibility, an advantage that auditing firms do not want to give up. In an ironic twist on what should be, auditing firms have a motivation to keep annual reports complex. It is more likely that reforms will eventually be generated by corporate leadership in cooperation with the stock exchanges. Each exchange devises and publishes listing standards; in fact, at the time that Sarbanes-Oxley was being drafted, the exchanges developed listing standards that formed the basis for many of the new rules. There is no reason that stock exchanges could not expand their influence over regulatory reform to improve communication via annual reports, requiring listed companies to adopt more specific reporting formats.

2. *Meaningful reform in the GAAP system.* The GAAP system itself is not centrally coordinated, but consists of many opinions, interpretations, and analyses published by the FASB, the AICPA, various boards and com-

mittees, and other industry and government associations. Reform takes time. But GAAP is so flawed that you cannot tell what a company has really earned without referring to the S&P core earnings for each company. You also cannot tell what the real tangible book value is for any corporation because so many major liabilities are excluded from the balance sheet, such as pension liabilities and the obligations of off-balance-sheet partnerships and subsidiaries. The fact that GAAP allows these material exclusions demonstrates that the whole system is ineffective. Real reform would have to include transparency, and that means that all assets and liabilities, at fair market value, should be shown on the balance sheet. The "core net worth" of a company may be as elusive as its core earnings, but it is just as important for investors to have this information.

3. *Enforcement of auditor conflict-of-interest standards, from the corporate side.* Since the passage of Sarbanes-Oxley, it has become evident that accounting firms will not reform themselves. The big firms appear to view the problems of the past decade as public relations issues rather than as intrinsic conflicts of interest. No serious call for reform came from within the industry, even though Sarbanes-Oxley took away the accounting industry's self-regulatory role and replaced it with an oversight board. Imagine how serious it would be if the federal government believed that the medical or legal profession needed to be supervised by a regulatory agency; it would create quite a shock. But this is exactly what Sarbanes-Oxley imposes on accounting firms. The only way to remove auditors' conflict of interest is through corporate action. Corporate leadership, including the CEO, the CFO, and the audit committee, needs to make it a policy that the company must use different auditing firms for its external audit and for all other accounting consultation. Only when this occurs can you believe that the annual report strives to provide you with real transparency.

4. *Restrictions on incentive compensation.* Among the many problems seen in public companies in the past was that of incentive compensation to executives. These large bonuses (often in the millions of dollars) and generous stock options were often granted on the basis of reported profits and stock price levels. This still goes on today. So executives have every incentive to exaggerate the company's profitability and future growth potential. Their own income is often based on how well the results get re-

ported. Under the rules of Sarbanes-Oxley, financial executives cannot have contact with auditors and the whole auditing process is supposed to be kept apart from the company's executives. But as long as executives continue to be paid on the basis of how profitably a company operates or how high its stock goes on the market, conflict of interest is possible. Reform should include limitations on executive *incentive* compensation if it is based on profits or stock prices. This type of reform, like so many others, needs to come primarily from within each company. However, the exchanges could also set minimum requirements as part of their listing standards.

5. *Disclosure of executive compensation as a section of the annual report.* Some companies include a section in the annual report showing salary and incentive compensation for the highest-paid executives and employees; most do not. But this type of disclosure is very useful. Stockholders have a right to know how much executives are paid, and, while pay levels are not specifically confidential, companies do not always make it easy for the public to find out that information. A truly transparent annual report would include the disclosure of compensation for all top executives and the highest-paid employees and directors. Although a lot of this information is found in the proxy report, most people only look at the annual report.

> **Key point:** Many corporations claim to believe in transparency. But a serious examination of annual reports, reporting formats, and the complexities of GAAP reveals that transparency remains elusive.

The idea of transparency in annual reports is a desirable one, a goal worthy of working toward. But it will require many changes beyond federal legislation to make it a reality. The process should begin where financial reporting begins, with the independent auditor. But the entire accounting industry and its culture do not operate in the interests of the investor. Chapter 8 explains the problem and how the industry needs to be reformed.

CHAPTER 8

THE AUDITING ROLE

ACCOUNTING CULTURE AND THE AUDIT MENTALITY

Investors make assumptions—especially when they see that a company's books are accompanied by an unqualified opinion by an outside auditing firm. That opinion is the key to trusting the numbers, or so it goes in traditional thinking.

An unqualified opinion is one containing language that blesses the books and records, stating that "in our opinion [the financial statements] present fairly, in all material respects, the financial position and results of operations" for the company for the years reported. Traditionally, this has been enough for investors and analysts. If the auditing firm said that everything was all right, you could depend on it.

As the whole market learned in 2001 and 2002, audit opinions were themselves under suspicion. So widespread were conflicts of interest among auditing firms that you could *not* rely on the unqualified opinion as you had thought.

▲ ACCOUNTING AND ACCOUNTABILITY— A PERSPECTIVE

The widely publicized involvement of Arthur Andersen—at the time one of the Big Five accounting firms—in the Enron situation rattled the entire business community and Wall Street. Among the accounting firms, Andersen's reputation was impeccable. Its founder had built the organization on a foundation of honesty and integrity. For many years, the firm's motto was "Think straight, talk straight."

Arthur Andersen founded his firm with partner Clarence DeLany in 1913. Until the 1980s, the firm continued to follow its leader's philosophy that an accountant's responsibility was to investors and not to the company being audited. In fact, this belief was an underlying assumption among the investing public throughout the entire twentieth century. In the 1980s, however, the competitive nature of the accounting and auditing industry led to a rapid unraveling of those high standards. It was not just Arthur Andersen whose standards fell; all of the Big Five firms were named as defendants in investor lawsuits and were investigated by federal and state regulators.

> **Key point:** Arthur Andersen's name is identified with Enron and with the worst accounting abuses. But in fact, *all* of the Big Five accounting firms were involved in questionable audits throughout the 1990s.

The problems began in the 1980s, when the industry began expanding its nonaudit services. Accounting firms continued providing "independent" audits for their clients, but they also provided internal system consultation, legal, bookkeeping, computer, and many other services. Ironically, it was Arthur Andersen that launched this departure from the past. Andersen was the first accounting firm to recognize the potential for nonaudit revenues, especially in connection with automation. Andersen used its connections with audit clients to generate nonaudit business.

The revolution in automated accounting services began in 1950, when Andersen introduced the Glickiac (a computer named for its inventor, Joseph Glickauf), which, for the first time, provided nonscientific civilian applications for computers. The idea that computers could be used for bookkeeping came from Arthur Andersen. By 1997, audit and tax revenues at Andersen were running at $1.8 billion, but nonaudit consulting had risen to $3.1 billion. Steve Samek was a senior Andersen partner who was named to head Andersen in 1998. He devised the company's so-called 2X strategy, a requirement that partners should generate two dollars of new business outside their practice area for every dollar they currently generated. So an audit partner generating $4 million per year in audit revenues was expected to create $8 million in nonaudit revenues as well. In fact, 2X became the basis of performance review at Arthur Andersen.[1]

By the 1990s, all of the large accounting firms were competing for nonaudit work. Andersen was the country's largest accounting firm, with 85,000 employees. But there had been problems. Questionable audit decisions—or, more specifically, a failure to challenge the corporate accounting misdeeds of many of its clients—brought the firm unwanted publicity regarding Andersen's role in either not disclosing accounting problems or going along with client decisions that violated the rules. These clients included Sunbeam (Andersen settled shareholder suits for $110 million), Waste Management (Andersen settled shareholder suits for $75 million), Boston Market (Andersen paid $10 million to settle), Baptist Foundation of Arizona (Andersen paid $217 million to settle a lawsuit), and finally Enron, for which Andersen was charged with witness tampering and obstruction of justice in June 2002, resulting in the firm's going out of business altogether.

Andersen was not alone in its involvement with questionable client practices. The other major accounting firms also faced a series of lawsuits, settlements, and failure to alert regulators or investors about misstated earnings and other deceptions. Throughout the 1990s, all of the Big Five firms were sued numerous times and were required to pay fines and settlements in dozens of cases.

Key point: Inadequate audit work is not just a thing of the past. Lawsuits and legal reform are desirable. But similar problems may be recurring today as well. There is no guarantee that the problem has disappeared.

All of this history points up the fact that the accounting industry had serious conflicts of interest. It was not only corporate executives with incentive compensation whose motives were questionable. For auditing firms and ambitious senior partners, it became virtually impossible to challenge a client's accounting practices as part of an independent audit; such a decision could lead to the loss of valuable nonaudit revenue and the end of a promising career.

As long as accounting firms provided audit and nonaudit services for the same clients, this conflict of interest remained. The higher the revenues became, the worse the conflict of interest. It was apparent to regulators that reforms in the law were needed to remove these conflicts, so that public trust in the auditing industry could be reestablished. This led to the passage of the Sarbanes-Oxley Act of 2002, which, among other matters, set up a new accounting oversight board and limited the services that accounting firms could offer to their audit clients.

The new rules sounded good, but they did not do away with the problem.

▲ SARBANES-OXLEY—TAKING OVER THE OVERSIGHT

Imagine the outcry if the federal government took over regulation of the legal or medical profession. If the government decided that attorneys or doctors were not doing a good job of self-regulation and assigned that task to a federal agency, it would be a dramatic change in those industries.

That is exactly what happened to the accounting industry in 2002. The Sarbanes-Oxley Act established a Public Company Accounting Oversight Board, a quasi-governmental entity. Its mission is to regulate auditors of publicly listed companies, and the board is supervised by the SEC. The very first paragraph of Sarbanes-Oxley (SOX) defines the board's purpose:

> To protect the interests of investors and further the public interest in the preparation of informative, accurate, and independent audit reports for companies the securities of which are sold to, and held by and for, public investors.[2]

This defining paragraph is a condemnation of the entire accounting industry, which—like the legal and medical fields, among others—had been a self-regulating industry until the new law went into effect. After repeated disclosures of violations, litigation, and the general failure of accounting firms to bring corporate clients into compliance, the new law became necessary.

> **Key point:** The accounting industry has changed only as much as the law requires. No meaningful reform has been generated from within the industry, and this is a serious problem for investors.

The accounting industry has reacted to the new law, but as a public relations problem rather than as an actual, internal conflict-of-interest problem. The industry is much larger than the remaining Big Four firms (PricewaterhouseCoopers, KPMG, Deloitte & Touche, and Ernst & Young). There are thousands of smaller firms available to corporations for the performance of audits and nonaudit work. However, the expectation that Arthur Andersen's problems would lead the remaining segments of the industry to improve corporate reporting and to promote transparency has not been realized. This goal—making corporate reporting easier to understand and entirely transparent even to the nonaccountant investor—is a central theme in the GAAP environment. The FASB defines the very purpose of its efforts based on the theme of transparency:

> Accounting standards are essential to the efficient functioning of the economy because decisions about the allocation of resources rely heavily on credible, concise, transparent and understandable financial information.[3]

It is true that economic health would be improved if investors were able to make sense of the financial information they have available. Most investors understand the basics of financial statements and how to apply a few ratios. But when it comes to working through the annual report, gaining useful knowledge from footnotes, and tracking the accounting assumptions through management's discussion, most people are lost.

The three main financial statements follow a very specific format and have done so for many years. However, there has been no attempt to make annual reports uniform, and that would be a simple matter. Footnotes should be presented in a prescribed order, with uniform titles, and containing exactly the same information, even among corporations. The sequence of annual report sections should also be uniform.

The accounting industry has not reformed itself, despite its having lost the right to regulate itself. This extraordinary change in an industry is very rare. But any real change in response to Arthur Andersen's history, to the new law, or to public perception has yet to occur. The problem, defined in 2002 by ex-SEC Chairman Harvey Pitt, remains unchanged. He noted, "Accounting firms have important public responsibilities. We have had far too many financial and accounting failures."[4]

The decision to include a new federal oversight of auditing firms in SOX came from the realization that accounting firms and the industry were failing in their role and not acting in the public's best interests. The high volume of lawsuits naming accounting firms and the huge dollar amounts of losses (including Enron, WorldCom, Lucent, and dozens of other companies whose audits did not disclose problems) contributed to the decision by the SEC and by Congress to remove responsibility for self-regulation from the GAAP community and the accounting industry.

Key point: The fact that self-regulation was taken away from the accounting industry provides insight into the scope of the problem. That itself is a major failure among accounting firms—a failure to protect investors from inaccurate accounting.

That industry resisted the enactment of reform through SOX from the beginning of the discussion. Only reluctantly has the industry accepted the new rules, and far from cooperating in reform, accounting companies have argued against most of the major provisions. The AICPA, for example, was strongly opposed to a suggestion that senior auditors should be rotated off a specific account at least every five years. The idea was that familiarity was not good for objectivity. The head of the AICPA argued, "The more I understand about a business, the better able I am to be critical in an audit."[5]

This point of view is contrary to what most people would believe. In fact, in order to remain objective in an independent audit, a senior auditor would be in a better position if he knew little or nothing about the

company, its employees, or its executives. The example of Arthur Andersen and Enron emphasizes this.

In the same speech, the AICPA head stated that a "rejuvenated accounting culture" was the solution.[6] However, that is an internal point of
view and self-serving for the industry. Rather than developing a rejuvenated culture, the industry needs to reexamine its own values and purpose. It has been charged with auditing companies on behalf of the
investing public. The audit firm works for the stockholders, not for management—and this is the crux of the problem. Accounting firms, having
become too involved with corporate management and generating audit
and nonaudit revenues in the billions, became (and remain) tied to those
corporations by a financial umbilical cord that will be difficult and pain-
ful to cut.

▲ THE SOX RULES

Sarbanes-Oxley addresses these problems by prescribing major changes
in how auditors work with their corporate clients, how auditing firms
are hired, and auditors' contacts within the corporations regarding audit
findings. However, it remains to be seen whether the changes in the law
will translate into better transparency and better quality in audit work
itself.

The framework for the reforms instituted in SOX was developed by
the SEC in cooperation with the New York Stock Exchange (NYSE). In
June 2002, the NYSE published its recommendations in a report called
"NYSE Corporate Accountability and Listing Standards." This included
specific recommendations to the NYSE board of directors involving
changes in the requirements that the exchange should impose on its listed
corporations. These changes were adopted and subsequently incorporated into SOX.[7]

The new law contains five specific and distinct sections. These deal
with the newly establishing oversight board, auditor independence, corporate responsibility, enhanced financial disclosures, and analyst conflicts
of interest. Additional sections are quite specific about the new requirements at all levels, with the purpose of ensuring full disclosure of material
facts, transparency in reporting, and, most difficult of all, removal of the

serious conflicts of interest on many fronts: accounting firms, corporate executives, individual analysts, securities and investment banking firms, and corporate board members.

The sections dealing with accounting firms are interesting because they impose new restrictions and prohibitions. The first section of the law involves the creation of the Public Company Accounting Oversight Board and its power to create and regulate standards for audits, quality control, and independence of auditors. One of the more interesting sections involves the question of "accounting standards." The act gives the newly established board the power to set actual standards, assuming that this role is to be filled by the FASB, with funding provided by Congress. The board's involvement strengthens the authority of a FASB standard by providing it with an SEC-acknowledged GAAP ruling. The reasoning behind this change was explained in the SOX Senate Report:

> The bill seeks to formalize the SEC's reliance on the FASB and to strengthen the independence of the FASB by assuring its funding and eliminating any need for it to seek contributions from accounting firms or companies whose financial statements must conform to FASB's rules.[8]

The section involving auditor independence establishes new rules designed to ensure that investors' interests are protected and removing conflicts of interest. The situation prior to SOX, in which auditors performed both audit and nonaudit work for the same clients, was a serious problem in itself, considering that senior auditors' careers depended on revenues. It was difficult for auditors to challenge a client's wrongdoing if that could lead to the firm's losing the client and the associated revenue. The larger the client, the greater the auditor's difficulty.

Key point: A truly independent audit would require complete objectivity by the auditor. As long as auditing firms rely on their audit clients for nonaudit revenue, that objectivity is impossible.

This reality created and *demanded* a conflict of interest on the part of the auditor. SOX addressed this problem in several ways:

1. *Accounting firms are prohibited from conducting audit and nonaudit work for the same clients.* At first glance, the SOX restriction on auditing firms performing nonaudit work seems quite strong. However, the law lists only nine prohibited activities, leaving room for firms to redefine or rename the services that they offer. A firm providing audit services may not also give the same client consulting services in bookkeeping; financial systems design and implementation; appraisal, valuation, and fairness opinions; actuarial services; internal audit services; management services; human resources services; broker-dealer services; and legal services.

Two types of conflict of interest exist when auditing firms provide both audit and nonaudit services. First, an auditor is going to be less likely to question or challenge accounting decisions for fear that her firm may lose the client. Second, when the firm provides nonaudit work, there is a likelihood that the accounting firm will end up auditing its own work. This section of SOX was intended to remove these conflicts of interest. But more reform is needed. Only a few months after SOX went into effect, the Big Four accounting firms had shown little change in their mix of business. By September 2002, all four firms continued raking in between $3 and $5 billion per year from nonaudit work, and the problem has not disappeared since then.[9] The numbers don't break down whether firms are performing work for audit clients, but the point is that the revenue numbers have not changed at all.

2. *Auditors report to the audit committee and not to the CEO or CFO.* In the past, corporate executives had complete control over which auditing firm was selected, how much it was paid, and whether or not to replace that firm. The same executives reviewed audit findings and negotiated any disagreements with the senior auditor. SOX required that the CEO and CFO have no direct control or hiring or firing authority over the auditor, or the ability to review the independent audit. That role was transferred to the firm's audit committee.

The committee itself was affected by SOX. This committee, which is responsible for appointing, compensating, and overseeing auditors, also receives reports from auditors and is in charge of resolving disputes between the company's accounting and audit determinations. Every member of the audit committee must also be a member of the company's board of directors. No member is allowed to accept fees for consulting or advising the company beyond his role as a board or committee member (thus, members of management cannot serve on the audit committee).

3. *Audit partners must be rotated off accounts.* Both lead and review partners on the auditing team cannot remain on a specific client account for more than five years. They must rotate off. This provision is aimed at avoiding an auditor's becoming too familiar with the internal workings of a company.

4. *Audits cannot be performed for a client when a manager of that company worked for the auditing firm during the past year.* A "cooling-off period" is imposed when corporations hire executives from their auditing firm. Historically, corporations hired executives from an auditing team with some frequency. For example, a senior auditor might be offered the job of manager of the internal auditing department. From a qualification standpoint, it made sense to hire an audit expert. But this practice also provided an insider's point of view to the "independent" audit mindset. Under SOX, an auditing firm is not allowed to audit a client if any of that client's senior managers have worked for the auditing firm during the past 12 months. The prohibited employment roles include CEO, controller, CFO, chief accounting officer, or any employee serving an executive role involving accounting and/or finance.

5. *Rotation of auditing firms may be required in the future.* The law also included a provision for the "study of mandatory rotation" of auditing firms. If this provision were ever made into actual law, a corporation would be required to change its auditing firm periodically.

Do these reforms make annual reports more transparent, more accurate, or less likely to contain misleading information? The problems with the annual report go beyond the complexities of the accounting rules. These GAAP rules have not changed significantly since the passage of SOX, and there remains enough flexibility in these rules for accountants and auditors to find justifications for all but the most questionable decisions.

Key point: Changes in the law designed to remove conflict of interest are a fine start. But with billions of dollars in revenue at stake, real reform must move beyond the law. The problems

> with annual report formats and content point out the reality:
> Real change has yet to occur.

For example, it remains possible to book revenues early or to capitalize expenses (methods for increasing the current year's income) or to defer reporting revenue (creating a "cookie jar" of earnings available for future periods when revenue and earnings would otherwise be low). These deceptive practices remain possible, and the rules affecting auditors do not prevent them. In fact, all of the changes merely create distance between the corporate accounting executives and the external auditors. None of the rules regarding actual accounting practice have changed. The annual report is prepared in each company without a standard format or sequence, the footnotes are not uniform, and the titles of specific footnotes and all other sections of the annual report vary from one company to another.

Web sites for different corporations also vary. In some cases, a link to investor information is easily found, while others require going to the site map or performing a search on "annual reports" to find the right link. Some sites (like Altria's) provide a table of contents for the annual report with links for each page, but others (like Kodak's) require you to click through every page in the 200-plus-page report.

▲ THE ACCOUNTING CULTURE

It may be accurately observed that accountants (whether they are auditing a client's records or working for the corporation) do not truly appreciate the difficulties that investors face in trying to understand their financial reports. And if they do understand this issue, they do not feel inclined to fix the problem.

The accounting culture is a sort of closed society, in which those who know how things work view the world as containing two types of people: accountants and all others. This is true, of course, in all specialized occupations, especially those with a high degree of technical expertise involved. So it is difficult for accountants to adopt a marketing or investor-sensitive point of view. This is why reform has to be imposed on the accounting industry from the outside. This was true with the reforms included in SOX, and it will also be true for any future reforms.

This culture is characterized by one important attribute worth considering when you think about reform: Accountants often do not comprehend the difference between disclosure and transparency. The accounting discipline emphasizes proving and documenting transactions, creating a paper trail, and verifying controls. In this environment, the perception of the end result is, "If you can prove it, the job is done." Lost in this process may be an outsider's understanding of the *meaning* of the transaction itself.

> **Key point:** Accounting is aimed at providing a methodical, orderly procedure for proving transactions and protecting companies against misuse of funds. But accounting is *not* an interpretive science, just a reporting system.

The accounting mentality permeates the entire process of documenting transactions, going through the audit, and putting together the annual report. The annual report itself is a strange hybrid, a combination of accounting and legal documents and public relations messages. The accounting side of the annual report places great emphasis on disclosure, whereas the public relations effort is aimed at casting the company in as positive a light as possible. Thus, the letter to shareholders—probably prepared by a public relations department—is invariably positive in tone, even if the numbers are dismal. However, this letter is normally placed near the front of the annual report to serve as an introduction to the disclosure documents that follow: financial statements, footnotes, and the auditor's letter.

It is apparent that the accounting point of view on the annual report is that the various disclosures (especially those provided in the footnotes) are acceptable efforts at transparency. They may be transparent to other accountants, but to everyone else, the footnotes are for the most part difficult to comprehend. They disclose, but only in a passive manner. There are no interpretive or instructive elements in footnotes. So when you read the lengthy "significant accounting policies" section normally found near the beginning of the footnotes, what conclusions are you to draw? How do these policies affect valuation or profits? What would the differences have been if the company had not followed the specific policies documented in the footnote?

These are important questions, and yet they remain unanswered. A truly transparent format for the annual report would include a complete discussion along with the disclosures. It would include educational elements demonstrating important financial ratios and also providing an honest discussion of negative trends. Most investors would find it quite valuable to read about a negative trend and, in the same report, find an explanation of the steps the company is taking to correct the problem.

The passive nature of the entire accounting format in the annual report provides disclosure without transparency. To fix this problem would require a complete change in the accounting culture, which is more *legalistic* in nature and not at all designed to assist investors in better understanding the companies whose stock they own. Even though auditors actually work for the investor, they perform more as though they worked for corporate management. The changes instituted in SOX were designed to change this. But a realistic change in the accounting culture may never occur unless it is imposed by corporate management. A simple solution would be for management to make its own reforms to the accounting culture, in at least four ways:

1. *Set a policy of separating audit and nonaudit work.* The simple decision by corporate management to use one accounting firm for audit work and a different firm for all nonaudit consultation would go a long way toward eliminating the accounting conflict of interest. The flaw in SOX is that it names a few services that auditing firms cannot provide to its audit clients, but since the law was passed, auditing firms have continued to offer the same consultation services, often to the same clients, but with different titles, or through subsidiary companies. There are too many ways around the law: offering the same services through subsidiaries, getting permission to offer services as exceptions, or simply renaming the services being provided, for example. Corporate management needs to recognize the mistrust of accounting firms as a corporate problem. By instituting a new policy doing away with the problem, management would provide a service to its investors at the same time.

2. *Identify and enact true transparency for investors.* There is no sub-
stitute for complete disclosure and education of the nonaccountant investor. Management needs to recognize that the existing format of the
annual report does not provide transparency to investors. True transparency would involve honest explanations of negative trends and preparation of footnotes with highlighted trend analysis (along the lines of well-
known ratios, complete with an explanation of what the company is
doing to continue positive trends or to reverse negative ones. This should
be done as part of the annual report and not as a function of the audit.)
In addition, operating statements could be provided in three different
formats. The *GAAP* format is the one currently provided, and is also the
least accurate. A *statutory* format would duplicate what the corporation
reports on its federal tax return. And a *core earnings* format would include
only core revenue and expenses, ending up with the core earnings as the
bottom line.

3. *Work toward a uniform format for annual reports.* There is no
sound reason for continuing the current system, in which annual report
formats are confusing and uncoordinated. Every company prepares its
annual reports on its own basis, using different titles for sections and
including specialized sections in different sequences. Corporate web sites
are similarly difficult to access. Some make links to annual reports easy,
and others are quite difficult to use. Every corporate home page should
include a link directly to "investor information," where an "annual reports" link should be easy to find. Changes in the current system and the
creation of a uniform format are most likely to come from the stock
exchanges, where these reforms could be made a part of corporate listing
requirements. Sadly, the accounting industry (where reform leadership
should reside) is out of touch with the investing public and seems unaware of the difficulty that people have in following the format and understanding the contents of annual reports.

4. *Change the internal accounting culture.* Corporate management can
make a significant change in the unending conflict between accountants
and the rest of the corporate world by changing the internal culture.
In most companies, two camps form: marketing and accounting. The
marketing attitude is that the "bean counters" emphasize documents and
never see a customer. Accountants view marketing people as "sloppy and

unwilling to provide documentation." Whereas each side has good arguments concerning the other, the unending conflict is not productive. A corporate philosophy should include the concept that every employee has a customer. Even the accountant, who never sees the *external* customer, prepares reimbursement, commission, and payroll checks for everyone in the company. In this regard, the accountant's "customer" is everyone who receives a check. A customer service culture could replace the existing "marketing versus accounting" culture that characterizes the internal corporate environment. Virtually every company experiences some form of internal, departmental, or segment-based conflict. These problems have a negative impact on the corporation's ability to pursue quality and to create a competitive advantage.

▲ CORPORATE SOLUTIONS

Accountants' view of "outsiders" is an impediment to reform. But the problem is not isolated to accountants. There is also a general unawareness on the inside of a corporation about how change would affect investors. A true level of transparency would attract investors to the corporation, and more people would want to buy its stock. Three factors that prevent this realization, currently, are:

1. *The perception that only big institutions count.* Those corporate executives who are aware of the interaction between the corporation and the investing public see the market from a very narrow point of view. By far the greatest volume of trades is executed by institutional investors (mutual funds, insurance companies, and pension plans), and retail investors—individuals—constitute only a small percentage of trading volume. Even though 90 million individuals invest in the market,[10] there is a tendency among corporate executives to be aware of the concentrated influence of a few institutional holders of large blocks of stock.

2. *Unawareness of the public relations advantages of honest change.* It is difficult for corporate insiders to grasp the significance of public perception. Few corporations are able to recognize the need for change or the impact that it will have. When some corporations announced in 2002 that they were going to begin reporting stock options as current expenses,

it was a bold move. This was not a requirement under GAAP (even though stock options can represent a significant expense), and these few leaders recognized the need to make the change voluntarily. This decision also provided these corporations with exceptional public relations benefits. The short list included General Electric, General Motors, Bank One, Procter & Gamble, and Coca-Cola.[11]

3. *Mistrust of the investing public.* Part of the corporate culture is based on the belief that investors will flee if they receive any bad news. Even underperformance in a single year—lower revenues than the previous year or declining earnings, for example—will cause investors to sell their stock, the belief goes. The desire by institutional investors to cut quarter-end losses often leads to weaker performance and selling positions for the wrong reasons, which is a disservice to customers owning shares. This motivates corporations to hype their annual reports, especially the "To Our Stockholders" section and other public relations sections. However, a frank explanation of an underperforming year would provide an exceptional opportunity for corporate management to explain how it is making changes to reverse negative trends. The problem with hype is simple: If the corporation never admits to any negative trends, there is no reason for it to explain how it is going to fix the problem.

> **Key point:** Corporate executives seem oblivious to the investor's dilemma, and to the need for complete, useful communication. Most people know when they are being fed slogans.

Investors know how to interpret general trends. When you see revenues declining over a decade, with ever-weakening earnings following, you know there is a problem. For example, when you review a 10-year history of Lucent and see revenues falling from their 1999 high to one-fourth that level by 2004, the negative direction of the trend is obvious. The "To Our Stockholders" section began with the positive comment that "Fiscal 2004 was a pivotal year for our company. For the first time since 2000, we posted a profitable year and achieved annual revenue growth."[12] It would have been refreshing if this opening had been more forthcoming, explaining that "Revenues, while up slightly from the year before, continue to be a fraction of the volume reported only a few years before." The explanation that followed could explain the reasons for the decline *and* the steps being taken to reverse the trend.

A negative trend is an opportunity for management to explain its current programs. Unfortunately for the investing public, corporate management is oblivious to this opportunity and sees its role as one of soothing a nervous investing public, providing a glowing report not only of the past year but of the future as well—even when the numbers tell a different story. For this reason, the letter from the CEO or president has to be largely discounted in any review of an annual report. If the news is good, the numbers are self-explanatory. If the news is bad, you are unlikely to find an honest explanation of it in the annual report. Until a broad change in corporate culture occurs, large numbers of corporations will not discuss the issues in a way that addresses the real problems.

To find an honest discussion of trends, you need to look to analytical reporting services such as the Standard & Poor's Stock Reports. For example, while the Lucent "To Our Stockholders" section provided a glowing, optimistic claim concerning growth in revenues (even though that growth consisted of only one year and was slight), the Stock Report provides a more realistic explanation: "We believe customer concentration has cut down on profitability with lower volumes during market downturns like 2001. . . . In our opinion, LU is at a competitive disadvantage to its peers."[13]

Imagine what the "To Our Stockholders" message *could have been* if it had presented the same negative information. It would then have provided an opportunity for the company to confront the problem and to explain how the company is taking steps to (1) improve profitability and (2) regain a competitive advantage. It may be that investors can accept bad news if the company provides, at the same time, a game plan for recovery. But the practice of always painting results in a positive light, no matter how bad the results, is a disservice to the investing public and an intrinsic problem with the annual report format currently in use.

▲ FINDING REAL TRANSPARENCY

In order for these changes to occur, corporate leadership will need to acknowledge the need for change. As long as there remains a widespread belief that the annual report as currently offered is adequate, no reform will be possible—at least, not reform generated from within corporations themselves.

Key point: The belief among corporate executives and accounting professionals that the annual report is just fine as it is presented is at the heart of the problem in corporate communication. The job simply isn't being done.

A second problem with the suggestion that corporate management can bring about change is that, with thousands of publicly traded companies, no single one would be able to propose and enforce a single standard. Corporate leadership can and should reform the conflict of interest that the entire accounting industry suffers from. It is clear that the accounting industry is unwilling to take the lead in reforming itself. However, although the accounting industry would be the logical center for fixing the annual report problem, it is an unlikely source for real change. The GAAP community is slow-moving, reluctant to adopt changes, and, worst of all, unwilling to admit that there is a problem. No suggestion that annual report formats need fixing has come from within the FASB or the AICPA.

Transparency should be defined on an expanded level. This new definition should include the need for uniformity in reporting standards and formats, clear explanations of even the most technical issues, and adoption of full disclosure of operating results using three different computation methods. All of these reforms should be incorporated into a revised format for annual reports.

The "letter to shareholders" section of today's annual report is worthless for any analytical purpose. It would make more sense to have this analysis provided outside of the corporation. But that is not a likely event. Investors need to look to research services outside of the corporation in the quest for an objective summary that is not as self-serving as the corporate version of a company's financial status.

There are many sections of the annual report that are of great value, but they are often hidden like so many Easter eggs—and it is your task to find them and place them into your information basket. The desirability of having all of the important information presented to you, including interpretations and explanations of current trends (positive *and* negative), is not likely to ever be accepted by corporate management. It is a great disservice to investors that the CEO and CFO do not willingly provide information in the format that would be most useful. This is why outside analysis is essential.

The fact that accountants restrict themselves to a passive assurance of the numbers (which is not reliable even as far as it goes) is one element of the problem. Management also fails to provide investors with an active explanation of valuation and operations, so that you need to rely on outside sources. Chapter 9 takes on this problem by explaining how the numbers can be manipulated to exaggerate earnings, presenting six ways in which accountants and management use the accounting system to falsify results.

HOW THE NUMBERS
ARE MANIPULATED

ACCOUNTING SHELL GAMES

The recent history of accounting fraud includes several specific methods and tricks. The corporate executives who put these plans into action often had the silent approval of their auditing firms, whose revenues from non-audit work often exceeded their audit revenues. The conflict of interest for auditing firms was glaring, and, in many instances, the problem continues to exist today.

The annual report contains a certification by the auditing firm that is supposed to guarantee the accuracy of the financial statements. It has become clear that this is not enough. Even after auditing firms have had to spend millions of dollars to settle stockholder lawsuits, the annual report has not been improved, and the elusive ideal of transparency has not been realized.

To understand why the numbers are manipulated at all, you first need to understand how executive compensation is structured. Much of an executive's income is based on the performance of the company's stock and on the company's profitability. So if a company achieves record earnings, the executive is granted a bonus. If the stock price climbs to record high levels, the executive can make millions by cashing in stock options.

This chronic problem cannot be undone by legislation. It has been suggested that executive compensation should be limited or that incentive compensation should be done away with altogether. But that would impose standards on free enterprise, and, in many cases, those incentives are earned. The executives you hear about who abused the system are a minority, but that minority can represent a great threat to your portfolio.

Under Sarbanes-Oxley, the CEO and the CFO are required to certify the results of operations reported in the financial statements and filed with the SEC. If an executive certifies the statements falsely, it can lead to both civil and criminal penalties. In addition, new stock option rules require executives to hold on to stock for a specified period of time following exercise of an option, preventing some abuses. Many corporations have also instituted their own rules requiring executives to buy and hold a number of shares based on their salary and years of service. So some reform has taken place. Even so, it remains possible for accounting fraud to occur in the future, and for auditing firms to go along with it.

> **Key point:** The audit of listed companies is one important element in ensuring the validity of the numbers. But realistically, auditing firms may go along with some types of manipulation. In the past, some extreme cases have occurred.

How can nonaccountants spot fraud? It is not easy, but the most popular methods of fraud do show up in trends, and you can spot them. It would be advantageous if professional analysts could be relied upon to spot problems for you and to warn you when a company's results appear suspicious. But at the height of the scandals, in the year 2000, the market was falling, but less than 1 percent of analysts' recommendations were to sell anything.[1]

The following sections demonstrate how misrepresentation is done, and how you can spot it through trends.

▲ THREE TYPES OF MANIPULATION

A corporation's results should follow a somewhat predictable path. Common sense tells you that trends tend to move in a predictable manner, and that related outcomes will move in the same direction. For example, if revenues fall but net earnings rise, that is surprising. It doesn't make sense.

Even with this obvious relationship between related numbers, ratios, and trends, the past has demonstrated that questionable outcomes are not always questioned. This is true for a number of reasons:

1. *Accounting is a passive activity.* The financial sections of the annual report come in two varieties. The first is the financial statements, which are prepared internally and checked by independent auditors, perhaps with certain adjustments being made. Both the internal financial activity and the independent audit are passive. In other words, emphasis is placed on verification of the numbers, not on telling you what it all means. There may be a general assumption that the management discussion and letter to shareholders sections fill this void and explain the numbers. But the hard fact is that management's narrative sections usually emphasize the positive and place a good spin on anything negative. Nowhere in the annual report do you find interpretive information. Most investors depend on the annual report to tell the "whole story" for the year, but they do not actually receive the kind of critical and balanced information that they need and want. Annual reports, sadly, are anything but transparent.

2. *Analysts do not understand fundamentals, as a rule.* Some investors, knowing that their own accounting knowledge is lacking, depend on the research and recommendations provided by analysts. The big Wall Street firms offer analysis to clients, including reports, target stock prices, comparative analysis, and recommendations to buy, hold, or sell stock. However, most analysts place their greatest emphasis on the technical side, the stock's current, historical, and future price. The closest analysts usually get to the fundamentals is an estimate of future earnings. In fact, actual earnings reports are usually judged as positive or negative based on how close they come to the analysts' predictions. This is a backward way of judging corporate performance. There are many cases where record revenues and earnings are seen to be negative because those earnings fell 3 cents per share short of the analysts' predictions. The service you buy may include fundamental information, but the emphasis is on the technical side. Beyond the analysts, there are a number of subscription services, such as Value Line and S&P. These services tend to rate investment risk

and to study both fundamental and technical trends in detail. The degree of actual financial interpretation varies, however, and a comparison of the actual basis for recommendations made by the various services can be a useful solution.

3. *Investors have historically trusted corporate management, audited financial statements, and analysts—at great expense.* The general sense of trust of the establishment is a feature of the Wall Street culture and has been for decades. However, it is undeserved. Many investors have lost their entire savings and retirement funds because they were given bad advice or defrauded. But each generation responds anew to the market in the same way. Waves of hysteria go in both directions. When the widespread belief is that a market can make people rich, the frenzy that ensues can be extreme. And when the opposite is true, a panic usually follows. In the seventeenth century, a craze for tulip bulbs took over the Netherlands market. With bulb values traded on the public exchange, many people became wealthy overnight, but when whole thing crashed, those same fortunes were lost. This was a case of investors wanting to believe in the value of something: The "experts" advised investing in tulip bulbs, and people mortgaged everything to buy them in spite of the illogic of it all. The same thing can happen in the stock market today, and the annual report, through which many investors are introduced to companies for the first time, serves as the starting point.

4. *Investors tend to be too trusting, even when faced with glaring contradictions.* The promise of great wealth is difficult to resist, even when logic would contradict the appeal. In 1919, Charles Ponzi set up an office in Boston and began promising 50 percent returns to investors in 45 days (and 100 percent in 90 days). By mid-1920, Ponzi was receiving $500,000 per day. People circled the block waiting in line to hand over their funds. The money was piled up in closets and in wastebaskets because Ponzi ran out of room. Nearly $10 million was paid in over one year. The impossibility of the promises was ignored in favor of the promise of easy money. Even after Ponzi was convicted of fraud, many people continued sending money to him in jail. Similar scams continue to this day. The relatively recent run-up in the value of Enron's stock is one of many examples. The run-up occurred even though the revenue and earnings results made no sense.

Key point: History tends to repeat itself. Those who chose to believe in Charles Ponzi were duped, but so were investors in Enron.

It is troubling that the whole system of reporting and analysis is so flawed. But that is only half the problem. Investors and their trusted advisers are attracted to the promise of fast wealth, and history has shown that people are easily deceived. The case of Charles Ponzi is exceptional because the fraud was so obvious; in more recent times, investors have been fooled by more sophisticated, better-hidden methods.

There are three general classifications of manipulation, beyond the outright theft of funds, that are likely to be uncovered. These are reporting exaggerated revenues and earnings, deferring earnings during exceptionally good years, and a range of manipulations that are both legal and allowed under GAAP but that are misleading.

Overstating revenues and earnings is done to maintain trends artificially, to bolster stock prices, and to convince investors that growth is better than it actually is. The same result—better earnings—is achieved when expenses are reduced or capitalized (set up as assets and amortized over many years). The opposite effect—reducing current revenues and earnings—is done to equalize results when the current year's earnings were exceptionally high. Deferring some earnings until later makes the trends appear more stable and less volatile than they actually are. This is a different type of deception, but it is still disturbing.

The most difficult type of deception to detect is that which is allowed under GAAP and practiced fairly commonly. For example, a company's decision to incur long-term debt primarily to maintain the current ratio level (even when revenues and earnings are falling) is a very deceptive practice. But there are no rules under GAAP and no laws that prevent corporate management from manipulating ratios and trends in this manner. In fact, the practice is rarely mentioned in management's discussion or letter to shareholders, or elsewhere in the annual report. Audit opinion letters simply verify that the numbers are correct; they do not comment on the decisions management makes to deceive investors and to create artificial trends. It is up to each individual to review the ratios and spot

these practices on her own, and then to draw conclusions about the real
risks of buying stock and the real growth potential of a company.

▲ METHOD 1: PRERECORDED REVENUE

The first and best-known method of cooking the books is recording revenue early. A basic premise of accounting is that related items should
appear in the same accounting period. For example, earning revenues
involves incurring costs and expenses, and all of these revenues and costs
should appear in the same year.

> **Key point:** Recording revenues early is a serious misrepresen-
> tation. But in applying GAAP, it is an easy deception to carry
> off under the guise of legitimate accounting "timing" decisions.

Two methods are used to justify prebooking revenue. The first is the
percentage of completion (POC) method. In this accounting method, a
portion of both revenue and costs is booked during a manufacturing or
construction period before finished goods are delivered to the customer.
This is legitimate in industries where the production period is exceptionally long, such as aerospace and certain types of construction. But the
system can be misused as well. POC accounting has been used in some
situations where it is not allowed; in other cases, it has been used aggressively. When POC is used, costs and expenses are supposed to be booked
along with revenues, but that is not always done properly. The result:
Revenues are not recognized in the same fiscal year as the associated costs,
so current-year revenues are exaggerated. Raytheon (www.raytheon
.com), for example, misused POC accounting in the late 1990s and ended
up having to adjust its revenues. A summary of the reported annual revenues for the 10 years ended 2004 and the moving average for those same
years makes the point. This comparison is shown in Figure 9.1.

The moving average, computed solely from the data shown on this
chart, and a growing average each year, makes it easy to identify the point
where revenues were overstated through the use of POC accounting.

A second procedure is called *bill and hold* accounting. Under this

Figure 9.1

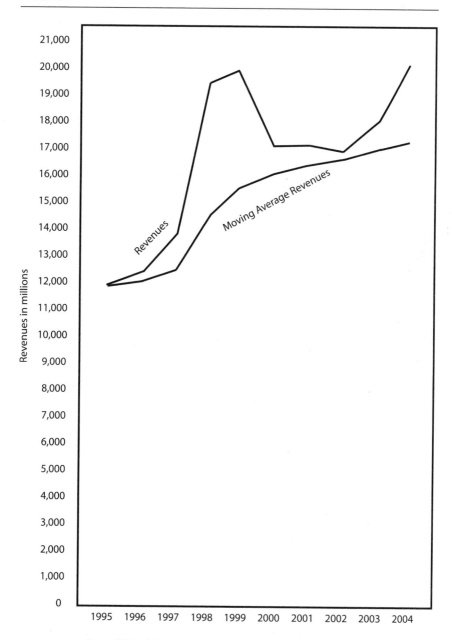

Source: S&P Stock Report, Raytheon Company, December 2005.

method, customers enter into a contract with the company to buy products or services in the future, often at a fixed price based on today's levels. The company keeps the goods in its inventory, and those goods are not scheduled to be shipped until later—for example, in the following year. However, the revenue is booked in the current year. A famous instance of this was Sunbeam. In 1996, the company presold its gas grills to customers up to six months before the following summer season. The level of this transaction was $35 million, and, when it was discovered, the company's auditor (Arthur Andersen) determined that the amount involved was not material.

Revenues can also be prebooked by shipping goods before customers expect them or by extending a year-end cutoff date. (Typically, companies close their books at or near the actual end of the fiscal year, but when companies want to inflate revenues, they may leave the books open for a few extra days.)

These kinds of tricks show up in several ways, and by tracking year-to-year ratios, they can be spotted. The things to look for include:

1. *Rapid growth in accounts receivable levels.* If you track accounts receivable levels in comparison to total sales, a pattern usually emerges. But if accounts receivable begin to grow as a percentage of revenues, that could be a sign that revenues are being booked in advance. If the company is achieving higher revenues with a journal entry only, the current ratio may also grow unexpectedly, making working capital appear artificially better than the facts justify.

2. *Surprising differences in year-end inventory.* If inventory levels change from one year to the next, this could be a sign of early shipment of goods, accompanied by early booking of revenues. Generally, inventory levels are determined by overall sales volume, so you would expect to see a predictable tracking level from year to year. When the levels change, it is a red flag.

3. *Unexplained increases in gross profit.* The manipulation of revenues to increase earnings in the latest year is difficult to hide on the operating statement. The gross profit (revenues minus cost of goods sold) has to increase when revenues are booked early. This occurs because the related costs are booked in the following year. Gross profit tracks revenues very

precisely; by definition, the cost of goods sold is directly related to revenue production, so any change in gross profit of more than a percentage point or two may be suspicious.

4. *Unexplained increases in net return.* Closely related to a suspicious gain in gross profit is an unexpected leap in net return. Most industries have a predictable and limited range of net return. Thus, if that return jumps from an established level of 8 to 9 percent per year to a surprising 13 percent, something is wrong. (Exception: If the mix of product lines or segments changed during the year, that change can affect both gross profit and net return. But if this has occurred, it should be explained in the segment reporting section of the annual report and in management's discussion and analysis. The lack of an explanation would be troubling.)

> **Key point:** All decisions to shift revenue or expenses from one period to the next are wrong if they violate this basic accounting rule: Revenues should be recognized in the year in which they are *earned*, and costs and expenses should be recognized in the year in which they are *incurred*.

When companies record revenues earlier than they should, this violates a basic accounting rule: All revenues should be booked in the year in which they are *earned*, and all costs and expenses should be booked in the year in which they are *incurred*. These matching transactions are essential to an orderly, predictable, and fair presentation of operations. So when companies book prerecorded revenues—even if their auditing firm considers the amounts involved to be "immaterial"—it raises many questions.

Even more serious is the case of booking artificial revenues. In this instance, the misdeed is taken up a notch. The way to discover this is to compare year-to-year changes in revenues and year-to-year changes in earnings. This information is readily available in the annual report. It is especially revealing when the two related trends do not track, but management provides no sound explanation. For example, when Enron's revenues grew by more than 250 percent in 2000 and earnings increased only 10 percent, the disparity was not explained by management. (Making matters worse, most analysts and mutual fund managers did not flag the problem either.) Because the revenues were not matched, questions should have been asked. The complex entries made by Enron in 2002 and preceding years finally came to light the following year, when the whole matter imploded.

▲ METHOD 2: MOVING EXPENSES TO LATER YEARS

There are two ways in which corporations can increase earnings in the latest year without involving revenues. These are capitalizing current-year expenses and deferring expenses until the following year.

When expenses are capitalized, they are set up as assets and written off gradually over a number of years through depreciation (normally and properly applied to physical assets) or amortization (used to write off prepaid assets like insurance). When expenses that would properly be recorded in the current year are capitalized improperly, it raises the net earnings for the year.

A second technique is a simple deferral of expenses. This can be done in two ways. Expenses may be recorded as assets at the end of the year, with the entry being reversed in the following year. This raises current earnings and moves expenses forward. Second, the company may put off recording expenses in the current year, even though they were incurred. This is a simple accounting trick. Normally, year-end unpaid expenses are recorded as accounts payable. Even though payment has not been made, the liability exists, and the expense is recorded as an accrual. But if the company simply fails to recognize the liability and expense, it is invisible and difficult to locate. Rent-Way (RWY) made a decision at the close of its 1999 fiscal year not to book year-end liabilities and their related expenses. The result was an artificial increase in 1999 net earnings of $28.3 million. The following year, the company repeated the practice, inflating earnings another $99 million.[2]

You can find these manipulations by observing several related trends: unexplained disparities in changes in revenues and earnings from one year to the next, increases in asset values in a single year (especially when those values fall back to previous levels in later years), and increases in depreciation for only one- or two-year periods.

Key point: If trends move in a surprising way, it could be a sign that the numbers were manipulated. That is usually the first hint.

For example, additional investigation would be justified from a review of Motorola's 1999 to 2001 results. Previous analysis discussed the growth in the debt ratio from 15.3 percent (at the end of 1999) to 39.3 percent (at the end of 2001). The increase in long-term debt was matched by increases in cash balances; and the current ratio remained level even though large net losses were reported (in 2001, the company lost $3.9 billion). However, the questionable numbers appearing on the company's financial statements did not end there.

Motorola's reported operating numbers for the two years 1999 and 2000 were also suspicious. A comparison between revenues and net income reveals an unexplained disparity in the changes between the two sets of numbers:[3]

		PERCENTAGE CHANGE	
YEAR	REVENUES	OPERATING INCOME	NET INCOME
1999	5%	9%	185%
2000	21	39	61

You would expect to see far less volatility in these accounts. Motorola's exceptionally high core earnings adjustments account for the differences between operating income and net income, but the problem involving revenues and operating income remains. When history reveals that in subsequent years, the company recorded large decreases in sales volume and drops in earnings, it brings up the question of what Motorola was up to in 1999, 2000, and 2001 (in terms of long-term debt, revenue policies, and expenses).

A similar question arose regarding Xerox Corporation. Revenues for 1999 were reported as dropping 1 percent; but net income *rose* by 143 percent. By 2001, several accounting problems at Xerox came to light.[4] The company was accused of recording revenues from the sale of future receivables, a highly questionable practice. Recording current income from any such future event is not allowed. The company also booked leasing revenue in current years even though it would not be earned until future years. And in 2000, the company overreported $119 million through improper classifications and failure to write off bad debts. Collectively, these practices led to inflated earnings for Xerox in 1999 and 2000, and the results of adjustments showed up in far lower net income numbers in later years (as well as lower stock price ranges compared to the 1990s).

The transfer of current-year expenses to later years is easily accomplished in the corporate accounting department. And in some cases (such as failure to properly record current expense liabilities), the practice is difficult to detect. So an auditor might overlook the problem on a small scale. But when hundreds of millions of dollars are involved, it is much more difficult to ignore.

Key point: Manipulation does not always involve entering numbers into the books. Simply failing to record year-end liabilities will also increase earnings. This is difficult to detect because the manipulation results from a *lack* of action.

The problem may begin when the accounting department defers recording expenses because departmental budgets are low and unfavorable variances would make the report look bad. Simply putting off the recording of liabilities may mitigate the problem in the current month, but the problem tends to grow over time. Once the practice becomes common for internal budgetary reports, extending it to final results is a fairly easy step—especially if the external audit does not challenge the decision or deems it to be immaterial.

These observations do not imply that corporate executives consciously set out to create deceptive financial statements. Internal pressures, budgets, reporting, and the ever-present desire to maintain positive reports and growing stock prices all conspire to pressure employees. And GAAP makes it easy to manipulate the numbers, as it gives companies the latitude to make internal decisions favoring the creation of positive outcomes. The results, as seen in annual reports, often are distorted, even if only to create and maintain favorable trends. From the investor's point

of view, the whole annual report format—including the eternally optimistic letter from the chairman—does little to address the question of
how the numbers come about.

▲ Method 3: Reduction in Liabilities or
     Not Recording Liabilities

Closely related to manipulation of expenses is underreporting of liabilities. Every transaction contains two sides, and if accrued expenses are
simply not booked at year-end, there are two results. First, expenses are
not reported, creating artificially higher net earnings. Second, current liabilities are also distorted, creating higher net worth *and* the appearance
of healthier working capital than is actually present. The current ratio is
directly distorted when current liabilities are left off the books.

When companies begin manipulating their operating results, it invariably leads to an accumulation of liability account balances. If a company understates this year's liabilities, those balances will be much greater
next year or the year after. Sunbeam eventually had to admit to its accrual
adjustments, by which time its initial $35 million adjustment had grown
to over $100 million for two years.

> **Key point:** The conclusion by an auditor that manipulation is
> "immaterial" is troubling. While $100 million may be a small per-
> centage of total revenue, the *practice* of misrepresentation is
> serious, and it should be taken seriously by the auditor, no mat-
> ter how small a percentage change it makes.

Xerox's actions in 1999 and 2000 led to an odd jump in both current
liabilities and long-term debt in the year 2001. These changes were the
result of the previous year's manipulations. By the time such issues show
up and the company has to make adjustments to its previous reports, the
problem has already occurred. Compare the historical outcomes for
Xerox in the years 1999 through 2004 to see how liability balances can be
adjusted, but later must be absorbed:[5]

	1999	2000	2001	2002	2003	2004
REVENUES ($ MIL)	19,228	18,701	17,008	15,849	15,701	15,722
OPERATING INCOME ($ MIL)	3,815	1,946	3,011	2,803	2,585	2,451
CURRENT LIABILITIES ($ MIL)	7,950	6,268	10,260	7,787	7,569	6,300
DEBT RATIO (PERCENTAGE)	67.1	78.9	82.5	82.0	65.1	52.1
CURRENT RATIO	1.5	2.1	1.2	1.4	1.4	1.7

These outcomes demonstrate why you need to look at the entire picture and at several trends to discover what is actually occurring in a company. Xerox revenues declined during this six-year period, and operating income, while not consistent, seemed to follow suit. The low 2000 results include a restatement for previously discussed overreported revenue and earnings. A more interesting trend is found in both the current liability and the debt ratio trends. Typically, the current liability levels were flat, but at the end of 2001, they rose considerably. At the same time, debt rose to 82 percent of total capitalization before retreating to its historical level, ending up at 52.1 percent by 2004.

The changes during these years in the current ratio don't make sense when you view changes in current liabilities. To see what really occurred, you need to review current ratio and the debt ratio together. You During this whole period, the current ratio changed very little. You may ask—quite rightly—how can this be? How could the year 2001's current ratio remain virtually the same as that of 1999 when current liabilities rose so much? But when you also look at the debt ratio, the answer becomes apparent.

Given the fact that revenues and earnings were disappointing, with a consistent decline over the time reported, the other trends—debt ratio, current ratio, and liability levels—did not seem to fit. The changes in liability levels may have several explanations; at the very least, the Xerox results deserve more investigation. The 2004 annual report begins with the statement: "2004 was another year of continued progress, excellent execution and accelerated marketplace momentum for Xerox." This claim is contradicted by the one-year results *and* by the longer-term trends. The chairman's letter is accompanied by several charts emphasizing positive outcomes, including one labeled "Return to Profitability." But the notes to the financial statements include no discussion or explanation of the company's current or long-term liabilities.[6]

Key point: When the president's message to stockholders contradicts what the numbers show, you have an early warning that management is not presenting the picture completely.

Underreporting of liabilities may be even more significant than the manipulations commonly practiced through the timing of closing the books or replacement of working capital with long-term debt. Unrecorded liabilities that are allowed under GAAP can even show that a seemingly solvent company has negative net worth. Until 2006, companies were not required under GAAP to report employee stock option liabilities, even though many of these were huge. For example, at the point that Microsoft announced that it was ending its stock option program, it made adjustments of $8 billion in 1999 and another $3 billion in 2000 to include employee stock option expenses. Those unreported expenses were accompanied by unreported liabilities of the same dollar amounts.[7]

The off-balance-sheet liabilities of some companies can be massive. Few can match the levels achieved by Enron, but the problem remains. GAAP does not require companies to report liabilities for pension obligations, long-term leases, and many other substantial matters. GAAP, far removed from the more accurate core earnings basis for reporting, allows very inaccurate reporting of liabilities and earnings. For example, shortly after Standard & Poor's created its core earnings adjustments program, the company made a startling announcement: It estimated that if all of the expenses and offsetting liabilities making up core earnings adjustments were reported in the financial statements and in annual reports, the overall earnings of the S&P 500 stocks would decline by 20 percent.[8]

▲ METHOD 4: CREATING HIGHER EARNINGS THROUGH NONRECURRING ITEMS

You will notice that there is often a glaring difference between operating income and net income. This difference consists of all nonoperating income or loss. It includes capital gains and losses, interest income and expense, and currency exchange adjustments. Also in this category are profits from the sale of operating segments, nonrecurring accounting adjustments, and one-time charges (often called "extraordinary" items).

> **Key point:** You often see big gaps between operating income and net income. That itself may not indicate a problem; but the reasons *should* be explained in the annual report.

Even though the distinction between operating income and net income is important and can be quite significant, this may not be highlighted in the annual report sections where the "good news" is being presented. These sections normally include the letter from the chairman or CEO and management's discussion and analysis of results. But when the gap between operating income and net income is wide, it may signal problems.

When you also compare GAAP-based earnings to core earnings, the differences often become even more disturbing. Compare the summaries of earnings using the different bases shown in Table 9.1.

The table shows that levels of reported income or loss are inconsistent and may swing widely from period to period. True transparency would and should include an analysis and explanation of these variations in the annual report, but management rarely even mentions the differences. And there are several levels of distinction in the reporting of profits. The difference between operating income and net income includes both nonrecurring items and nonoperational sources of income and expense. The fact that material differences occur in many of these values is confusing and deserves explanation by management. Even highly successful companies like Wal-Mart (www.walmartstores.com) show vast differences in these levels of income, although very little adjustment is needed to arrive at core earnings:[9]

| | FISCAL RESULTS (IN $ MILLIONS) | | | |
	2005	**2004**	**2003**	**2002**
OPERATING NET EARNINGS	18,729	16,525	15,075	15,367
NET EARNINGS	10,267	8,861	8,039	6,671
CORE EARNINGS	10,267	8,861	7,955	6,592

TABLE 9.1   EARNINGS COMPARISONS.

| Company | In millions of dollars | | | |
	2004	2003	2002	2001
General Motors				
Operating net earnings	$27,324	$26,423	$18,078	$12,853
Net earnings	2,805	2,862	1,736	601
Core earnings	4,047	4,510	(838)	(3,209)
Eastman Kodak				
Operating net earnings	$1,638	$1,685	$2,898	$1,923
Net earnings	81	238	793	76
Core earnings	(119)	149	127	(541)
Xerox				
Operating net earnings	$2,451	$2,585	$2,803	$3,011
Net earnings	776	360	154	(109)
Core earnings	666	434	(128)	(931)
Motorola				
Operating net earnings	$3,887	$2,694	$2,059	($2,595)
Net earnings	2,191	893	(2,485)	(3,937)
Core earnings	1,899	164	(2,084)	(4,893)

Source: Standard & Poor's Stock Reports, December 2005, for each company shown.

You can draw two conclusions from this and from Table 9.1. First, the differences between operating income and net income are substantial and deserve analysis within the annual report (in Wal-Mart's case, the difference consists primarily of provision for income taxes and interest expense). Second, the level of adjustments for core earnings is also important. The greater the adjustment, the greater the problems related to unreported liabilities, one-time adjustments, and nonrecurring items. You will observe that companies whose fundamentals are volatile also tend to have higher core earnings adjustments *and* high volatility in their stock trading range. By the same argument, those companies with consistent trends in revenues and earnings that also have low core earnings adjustments tend to report consistent growth in the stock's market value. This generalization makes the point that when earnings are provided by nonrecurring items, the overall trends have to be studied. The level of core earnings adjustments is useful in determining how much a company has used nonrecurring items to control its reported profitability.

▲ METHOD 5: REVERSE TECHNIQUES

Emphasis is usually placed on corporations' prebooking of revenues or deferring of expenses to *increase* current-year income. But some corporations have actually deferred earnings until a later period. The purpose of this has been to smooth out trends. So in an exceptionally successful year, the company may decide to "save" some revenues and profits until later. This practice has been given various names, such as "cookie jar accounting" or "sugar bowling."

> **Key point:** There is a tendency to think that bolstering the numbers is bad, but understating the numbers is acceptable. However, both practices are deceptive and should cause the same level of alarm.

Some analysts consider this practice relatively benign. When companies exaggerate revenues and earnings, it deceives investors. But when a company understates the same numbers, what harm has been done? In fact, both practices are troubling because they produce distortions, whether the numbers are moved in one direction or the other. It may be true that investors are comforted by predictability, but a consistently applied standard is always the best. And once it becomes "acceptable" to defer good news, it becomes just as easy to defer bad news—and the justification is often the same. The same basic rule applies: All revenue should be reported in the period in which it is earned, and all costs and expenses should be reported in the period in which they are incurred. Not only is this a basic accounting principle, but it is also a universally recognized GAAP concept.

Even though actual outcomes may be more chaotic than investors and analysts would like, any practice that distorts the numbers is troubling. But these matters are rarely discussed in the annual report. The practice can be recognized when certain balance sheet accounts change unexpectedly. The common practice in deferring revenues is to reduce the revenue numbers and offset them with a "deferred credit." This is a balance sheet oddity. It is included with liabilities, even though it is not actually a liability. So you may see a balance sheet reporting three groups:

current liabilities, long-term liabilities, and deferred credits. The subtotal of these is added to the stockholders' equity accounts to arrive at the total of liabilities, deferred credits, and stockholders' net worth.

The simple deferral of revenue by moving it into the liability section of the balance sheet is rather obvious. A bit more subtle is the practice of setting up higher than justified reserves. For example, in an exceptionally high-volume year, the company might increase its reserve for bad debts and its reserve for inventory obsolescence, to name two logical choices for building the cookie jar. Because those reserves are known to be too high, future additions to reserves can be correspondingly lower. The result: Earnings are deferred until they are released in a later period, *and* the documented justification can be made to sound reasonable. As long as a convincing argument is made that *at the time* the company believed that it needed higher reserves, it can always changes its mind later.

W. R. Grace, a chemicals and materials company that filed for Chapter 11 in 2001, tried to manipulate its numbers during better times. The company set up reserves in the early 1990s to defer unexpectedly high growth in revenues; by 1992 those reserves were at $50 million. A similar problem occurred in the 1970s and 1980s at H. J. Heinz. The company had set up a program for incentive compensation based on profitability, but once an annual ceiling was reached, bonuses were capped. Heinz managers may have withheld "excess" revenues and prepaid expenses to control earnings so that their bonuses would be maximized each year.

Microsoft also has used reserves to defer "excess" revenues during exceptionally good years. In 1998 and 1999, for example, the company increased reserves on its balance sheet and later reversed them into revenue.

Key point: There can be a fine line between proper and improper reserve accounting. The determination of an "appropriate" reserve level is subject to interpretation, so it is difficult to call the practice outright deception unless it goes to an extreme.

Whether companies exaggerate their revenues or defer revenues in bonanza years, the net result is that investors and analysts are misled. It may even be that corporate management does not intend to deceive any-one and believes that it is responding to investors' desire for predictability and steady growth. But the practice of cookie jar accounting is still wrong, not only under accounting standards, but also according to the law. While Heinz and Microsoft have not been accused of wrongdoing, the SEC did sue W. R. Grace in 1998, claiming that Grace had diverted as much as $20 million into reserves in 1991 and 1992.

▲ METHOD 6: DISTORTIONS ALLOWED UNDER GAAP

A final observation concerning distortion of results involves a broad set of techniques that companies use to make trends appear stronger than they really are. A popular technique involves reducing current liabilities (when cash flow permits) to maintain a healthy appearance for the cur-rent ratio. When cash flow is not adequate to "fix" a weak current ratio, some companies have simply accumulated long-term debt and kept the funds in cash. This increases the asset side of the current ratio, so that it remains consistent even in periods when revenues and profits are down. Consider the previous examples of Motorola and Xerox. In both in-stances, substantial increases in the debt ratio were accompanied by higher balances in current assets, even though revenues and earnings were weak.

Conceptually, there is no problem with a company's decision to in-crease its long-term debt, but this assumes a classic utilization of funds. If a company is using long-term debt to create permanent long-term growth (through expanded plant and machinery, acquisitions of competi-tors, and purchase of other permanent assets), management's decision may be justified. But if the growth in debt capitalization is undertaken solely to bolster trends used by analysts and investors, it is a disturbing abuse of the accounting rules.

Key point: Most people don't realize how limited the GAAP rules are. The rules do *not* include opinions as to whether man-agement's decisions were justified; they involve only the study of whether the transactions made (within those decisions) were proper and documented.

GAAP does not disallow such practices. In fact, GAAP rules apply only to how transactions are treated: the timing of recognition, classification of transactions, and such matters. So the auditing function checks transactions and applies GAAP rules to ensure that the presentation of the financial results shown in the annual report is in conformity with GAAP. The audit does *not* examine the justification for decisions made by management regarding the use of debt capital, when and how to acquire or sell assets, or the timing of payment of current liabilities to control working capital ratios. GAAP does not set up performance standards for the corporation; it only verifies that what the company claims occurred did, in fact, occur.

The lack of standards for transparency in corporate reporting is not solved or even addressed by GAAP. If corporations undertake one of the types of manipulation that violate the law, the audit should challenge the company and demand that adjustments be made to report the results accurately. In fact, when such practices are uncovered, a majority of audits probably do result in such adjustments. The audit process may find and fix many such problems, but the appropriate work of auditors rarely makes the news. You are most likely to hear about the manipulations that were not discovered until later, especially those where an auditor should have said something but did not. This is why so many of the lawsuits filed in the 1990s and through to 2003 involved accounting firms as well as corporations. When auditing work does not result in fixing manipulated numbers, the accounting firms are liable along with their clients.

The troubling aspect of GAAP goes beyond the historical complacency of accounting firms, working along with their clients to allow liberal interpretations and even outright misrepresentation in some instances. The problem is deeper. It is assumed that GAAP provides assurances that the numbers are correct, and so investors and analysts tend to trust the ratios and trends based on those numbers that they study. But because corporations have great latitude to use timing to create favorable ratios, it is necessary to apply a more comprehensive approach in your analysis, including:

1. A review of the key ratios over several years

2. Expansion of the review process to examine several factors collectively

3. A conclusion that all is not well when the combined analysis simply does not make sense (steady current ratios when earnings are falling, a rising debt ratio, suspicious changes in current asset and current liability levels between periods, and large differences between net earnings and core net earnings)

The annual report contains the basic elements for building your analytical program. But it is cryptic, like a jigsaw puzzle without straight edges. Until the whole organization of annual reports is reformed, you need to look beyond what the company and its auditors provide in passive form. Chapter 10 provides ideas for additional sources of the information needed to make wise investment decisions.

SOURCES OF FREE
INFORMATION

YOU DON'T NEED TO PAY FOR HELP

The common *perception* of the annual report is incorrect. It is viewed by investors as a document that provides all the information they need to make smart decisions. The question of whether to buy stock in a company can be based on a complete reading of the financial and other sections of the annual report, the belief goes. But you do not always find the transparency, interpretative analysis, and consistency of data that you need.

This perception—that the annual report provides everything that investors need—would be true if listed companies used a consistent format and if long-term data were provided as well. Part of the confusion concerning the financial information provided stems from the lack of a consistent format. For this reason, you probably need to supplement the annual report with additional resources.

> **Key point:** A lot of good information is found in the annual report, but at the same time, a lot is left out. At the very least, investors deserve consistent formats among all exchange-listed companies.

If and when listed companies do achieve transparency and unify the reporting formats of annual reports, the task of picking stocks and evaluating companies on a continuing basis will be far easier. Until that occurs, you need to accept the fact that annual reports are lacking. The information (or most of it) can be found in the annual report, but in cryptic form and with highly technical explanations.

▲ ONLINE RESOURCES

A wise place to begin looking for additional resources is the Internet. A vast array of free information can be found online, including four categories that are especially useful in trying to learn more about a company's valuation and operations. These are financial news sites, online brokerage services, tutorial and information sites, and free annual report services. A caution, however: There is also an abundance of unreliable information online.

1. *Financial news.* Many online services provide free daily financial news. Any of these can be set as your home page or set up as a desktop shortcut. A list of popular financial news sites is provided in Table 10.1.

TABLE 10.1   FINANCIAL NEWS WEB SITES.

Bloomberg	www.bloomberg.com
BusinessWeek	http://businessweek.com
CNN	http://money.cnn.com
Financial News	www.financialnews.com
Forbes	www.forbes.com
Fortune	www.fortune.com
Kiplinger	www.kiplinger.com
Lycos	www.quote.com
Market Watch	www.marketwatch.com
MSN	http://moneycentral.msn.com/investor
MSNBC	www.msnbc.msn.com
Reuters	www.reuters.com
Smart Money	www.smartmoney.com
The Street	www.thestreet.com
USA Today	www.usatoday.com/money
Wall Street Journal	http://online.wsj.com
Yahoo!	http://finance.yahoo.com

2. *Online brokerage services.* The problem with picking an online brokerage service is that the fees charged by different services cannot always be compared. Some sites offer a flat fee for equity trades, but when you read the fine print, you discover that the fees are higher for higher-volume trades and that separate fees are assessed for options trades, mutual funds, and ETFs. If you trade online, you may begin by comparing discount brokerage services. The use of a financial planner or commission-based stockbroker can be quite expensive, and many people have discovered that they are better off doing their own research and seeking low-cost trades. With online brokerage and quotes widely available, the need to pay $150 and up for stock trades is rapidly fading.

Fees for different brokerage sites are also difficult to compare because different sites offer a variety of services beyond trading. For example, Charles Schwab charges more than other discount brokerage companies, but it provides free S&P Stock Reports, Reuters Research, and its own Schwab Equity Ratings. These extra features make Schwab a bargain compared to the cost of far cheaper trading and separate subscriptions to the research services. Table 10.2 provides information on five discount brokerage services.

> **Key point:** A comparison of trading costs should not be limited to the simple cost itself. You also need to compare the free services that each brokerage provides to its subscribers.

3. *Tutorial and information sites.* Numerous sites provide free information, investment links, and extensive glossary entries. Stock exchange sites also provide valuable information about the exchanges, their listing

TABLE 10.2   DISCOUNT BROKERAGE WEB SITES

Name	Advertised Fee per Trade	Web Site
Ameritrade	$10.00	www.ameritrade.com
E*trade	$6.99 – $9.99	www.etrade.com
Charles Schwab	$12.95	www.schwab.com
Scott Trade	$ 7.00	www.scottrade.com
T. D. Waterhouse	$ 9.95	www.tdwaterhouse.com

requirements, supervision, and links to member companies. Although all of these sites offer some free data, they may also promote subscriptions to more extensive services. A listing of tutorial sites and stock exchanges is shown in Table 10.3.

4. *Free annual reports.* Virtually every listed company provides free annual report downloads from its corporate web site. Links to those web sites can be made found at online brokerage services or through stock exchanges. In addition, several free services provide the same downloads. Table 10.4 provides a list of several of these free services.

> **Key point:** Every listed company offers free annual reports, and it is easy to find these online. No one who has an Internet connection should suffer from lack of information.

▲ CORPORATE WEB SITES

Listed companies are normally accessible online and have web sites that provide important resources for investors: stock news and updates, annual reports, filings with the SEC, and product or service information.

TABLE 10.3   TUTORIAL AND INFORMATION WEB SITES.

Name	Web Site
Information and links:	
Daily Wall Street	www.dailywallstreet.com
Investopedia	www.investopedia.com
Money Page	www.moneypage.com
Morningstar	www.morningstar.com
Motley Fool	www.fool.com
Online Investor	www.theonlineinvestor.com
Quicken	http://quicken.intuit.com
Exchanges:	
New York Stock Exchange	www.nyse.com
Nasdaq	www.nasdaq.com
Philadelphia Stock Exchange	www.phlx.com
American Stock Exchange	www.amex.com
Chicago Stock Exchange	www.chx.com
Toronto Stock Exchange	www.tsx.com
Chicago Board Options Exchange	www.cboe.com

Table 10.4 Free Annual Report Downloads.

Name	Web Site
Annual Report Service	www.annualreportservice.com
AnnualReports.com	www.reportgallery.com
Investor Relations Information Network	www.irin.com
Public Register's Annual Report Service	www.prars.com
Wall Street Journal	http://wsjie.ar.wilink.com

Any corporation's web site can be accessed through a name search online or through an online brokerage service. With a brokerage service, you need only type in the trading symbol where indicated on the service's site. If you don't know the trading symbol, type in the name in the "symbol lookup" section. The stock exchanges also provide a link to each listed company:

The New York Stock Exchange (NYSE) (www.nyse.com) provides a home page link to "listed companies" and, from there, to a "listed company directory" that contains an alphabetical list of names and links for every company listed on the exchange. The link takes you to a summary page with the latest price and volume information, the trading symbol, a web site link, product descriptions, and additional links for investor relations, corporate profile, executives, financial information, and news releases. The "investor relations" link normally goes directly to a secondary link to annual reports, quarterly financial statements, and SEC filings, as well as to further contacts within the corporation.

NASDAQ (www.nasdaq.com) provides a similar section of "investor tools" links. This includes an "annual reports" link that takes you directly to a page where you can type in a trading symbol, a search, or a sublink by sector. A "listed companies" category on the home page provides a link to "national market list," which also takes you directly to listed companies' home pages and annual reports.

The American Stock Exchange (AMEX) (www.amex.com) shows a home page index with a subclass for "listed companies." Here a "company lookup" and complete alphabetical listing take you directly to the web site for each listed company.

> **Key point:** Exchange web sites are useful in many ways. They provide links to all member companies, where annual reports can be downloaded or read online. They also explain their listing requirements and supervisory actions.

It is easy to get to the web site for any publicly traded company on the U.S. exchanges through the exchanges themselves or through online brokerage services. Each of those links provides annual report summaries in most instances, although the method of finding annual reports varies considerably. Some web sites have an "investor resources" link right on the home page, while with others you need to do a site search. A few companies provide summaries only, requiring you to request annual reports by mail, but this practice is gradually being replaced with the more common PDF-format online annual reports.

On each corporate web site, a variety of internal contacts are also provided. If you have questions about an annual report, you can easily find the contact name and telephone number (and often an e-mail address) for the shareholder services department.

▲ PROFESSIONAL ADVICE

The Internet has made it easy, fast, and cheap to find all of the raw data you need to learn about listed companies. This does not mean that the information is well organized or easy to understand. But in the past, before widespread use of the Internet, it was impossible to get immediate access to information. Investors had to send away for annual reports and wait for them to arrive by mail or depend on a stockbroker to provide annual report information directly (again, usually waiting for mail delivery).

Today, individual investors are increasingly seeking discount brokerage services and getting research separately. Many brokerage services—including discount brokers—provide some form of free research online. So rather than paying steep trading fees to a traditional full-cost brokerage company, finding free research makes more sense for many people. It is becoming more and more the rule that if you invest directly in the stock market, you are unlikely to benefit from paid-for advice. And if you do continue to rely on advice, it is more likely that you will select mutual funds or ETFs (exchange-traded funds) rather than directly owned stocks.

Key point: The dismal history of paid-for advice from Wall Street firms contradicts the claims that these services are valuable. Today, investors are seeking low-cost trades and separate research, which also makes more sense.

To find a professional adviser if you need advice, a good starting point is a personal recommendation. But if you want to search in your area, contact the Financial Planning Association (http://www.fpanet.org). This industry association licenses and regulates industry professionals through the Certified Financial Planner (CFP) license. The web site provides a "find a planner" link where you can be put in touch with FPA members in your area. The CFP license is not easy to get. The FPA administers a certification examination and also requires three to five years of professional experience before the individual gets the CFP, and there are continuing education requirements as well.

When you pick a planner to advise you, determine how the person gets paid. Some planners call themselves "fee-based," meaning that they charge an hourly consultation fee, and others are paid by commission. A planner who gets a commission is going to recommend that you buy products that, in fact, pay a commission, so you are not going to be directed to a no-load mutual fund, for example. A fee-based planner is likely to be more objective in giving you broad-based advice that may include stocks, mutual funds, real estate, and other products. You will also want to ensure that a "fee-based" planner does not also receive commissions. In that case, you are paying for the advice, but the planner also gets a sales commission. This is the worst of all situations, because the planner is receiving two forms of compensation: She collects an hourly fee but still has an incentive to direct you to the products paying the highest commission.

Another important test in picking an adviser is to determine that person's knowledge level and how and why he recommends specific companies. You want to ensure that a planner knows how to study the annual report and is comfortable with the fundamentals: financial statements, ratios, and all the sections of the annual report. Among the services you should expect to pay for is an expertise in these fundamentals. Responsible investors should think of a planner's advice as a first step only, however. Once a planner makes a series of recommendations, you should still download and read the financial statements and check free analysis services such as the S&P Stock Reports, where you can review an entire decade of financial history.

If a planner expresses no interest in the fundamentals and wants you to simply take her advice—or emphasizes stock price only—then you should be aware of the distinctions. A technical orientation, basing investment advice on price alone, is not going to be as valuable as the advice from a financial planner who is an expert at reading and interpreting financial statements.

> **Key point:** You may believe in using fundamentals as a starting point in picking stocks. But many advisers do not know how to analyze financial statements and would prefer to steer you to mutual funds.

You may find that many financial planners do not provide detailed financial analysis as part of their service. In fact, a large number will discourage you from buying stocks directly, preferring to direct you to load mutual funds. This occurs because (1) commissions on funds are higher and (2) many financial planners' broker-dealers do not provide direct "wire service" (trading on exchanges) for their members, and that activity yields a very low commission. Planners often view stock business as high-maintenance—another reason why an increasing number of individual investors are moving away from paid financial services and executing their own trades online through a discount service.

▲ INVESTMENT AND SUBSCRIPTION ORGANIZATIONS

It is also worthwhile to look into joining one of two investment organization, the benefits of which include the research services available to members:

The National Association of Investors Corporation (NAIC) (www
.betterinvesting.org) has been around for over 50 years. It was
originally formed as the National Association of Investment
Clubs, but it provides broader investment services today. The
association has nearly 200,000 members in about 18,000 chapters
and is the largest investors' organization in the United States (it
also has many overseas clubs). The association also publishes *Better Investing* magazine.

The American Association of Individual Investors (AAII) (www.aaii
.com) was founded in 1978 and has 150,000 members. The association publishes the *AAII Journal* and provides members with
other publications and resources.

Key point: Investors may gain more knowledge through membership in an association than they could ever expect from a full-
commission broker.

Subscription services are usually used by individuals to find viable stocks or to track stocks that they already own. As previously mentioned, some services are provided free of charge to
people with open accounts with online trading services. Brokerage firms offer an array of newsletters and research reports for
a fee. The following are some additional research services worth
reviewing:

Value Line (www.valueline.com) offers its Investment Survey, a ranking of 1,700 stocks in more than 90 industries. The nicely detailed
rankings provide a combination of fundamental and technical
analysis and three- to five-year growth projections. The cost is
$65 for a 13-week trial or $538 per year. So it is expensive, especially if you can get most or all of your market analysis free from
an online brokerage service. Value Line is an excellent research
provider, but it is aimed at high-volume investors.

Morningstar (www.morningstar.com) analyzes 1,600 stocks for its
members and competes with Value Line in its coverage, detail of

information, and cost. Morningstar also ranks and rate mutual funds and costs $13.95 per month or $125 for a full year.

Standard & Poor's (www.standardandpoors.com) offers a number of equity research services, including the Standard & Poor's Stock Appreciation Ranking System (STARS) rankings and analysis of 1,500 U.S. stocks and 300 non-U.S. stocks. The online information does not provide subscription rates.

Zacks (www.zacks.com) provides a combination of free and paid subscription services online. It offers a free e-mail newsletter, industry rankings, and forecasts, and also offers the Zack's Equity Research service for a fee. The online information does not provide subscription rates.

> **Key point:** Generally speaking, paid research services provide a level of information that can often be found without charge through many online brokerages. A comparison is worthwhile, and your decision should be based on your trading volume and overall cost comparisons in each case.

▲ IMPROVING YOUR KNOWLEDGE BASE

The annual report is intended as the source document for everything you need to know before you buy stock. Unfortunately, it is prepared inside the corporation and often is a self-serving promotional document rather than a disclosure report. This disservice to investors makes it necessary to look beyond the annual report.

For example, the free analytical reports that you receive with some brokerage accounts are invaluable. They provide consistent 10-year results and include many important ratios. This level of information is often excluded from annual reports. Only a few companies provide more than five years' information (many provide only three), and the information you find in the key financial data is anything but consistent among companies. So if you, like many investors, recognize the value of comparative study of corporations, annual reports provide only part of the whole picture.

Your decision to use outside services, free online resources, or membership associations to augment your knowledge depends largely on the type of detail you need in order to make decisions. Some investors try to time their purchases and sales based solely on stock price movements and price charts. This technical approach is widely popular, even though it ignores the short-term chaotic nature of the market. At the other extreme is the detail-oriented fundamentalist who uses long-term trend movements and subtle changes in ratio relationships to make informed decisions. So while the technician is able to act quickly but with questionable raw data, the analytical financial investor may spend too much time and effort lost in the details.

Somewhere between these extremes is a balanced approach. By restricting your analysis to a few key ratios, you can gain a lot of information from annual reports and supplement that with a review of the S&P Stock Reports and similar research material. The annual report adds even more to your knowledge base when you know what to look for. Whereas all sections may provide insights, it is clear that the letter to stockholders is often purely promotional and may even contradict what the numbers reveal. So unless you accept the premise that a one-year upward movement after a decade-long earnings slide is a "return to profitability," you will view this and similar sections as what they are: pure promotion without any substance and often lacking a true interpretation of the facts. The valuable sections for the fundamental investor are the financial statements and footnotes. Special attention needs to be paid to the disclosure sections, including segment information, contingencies and commitments, and significant accounting policies.

Key point: You need to study annual reports to get a good sense of a company's financial condition. But to get a long-term history and to compare financial results between companies, you probably need more.

For example, when you see that overall revenues have fallen over the past three years, does that mean that the company's financial and competitive position is on the decline? A study of segment information might reveal that a major operational segment was sold or that a specific line of business is being gradually phased out. (Both of these possibilities describe the revenue trend at Altria, for example, which sold off its Miller Beer segment and booked declining domestic tobacco revenues over a period of years.) A study of contingent liabilities can also reveal potential effects on future profitability. For example, both Merck and Altria have needed to make very detailed explanations of many contingent liabilities, as both have been named as defendants in literally thousands of lawsuits.

Anyone who studies annual reports in detail knows that good information can be found within their pages. At the same time, these documents could be vastly improved. The next chapter offers suggestions for the types of reform that are still needed to achieve real transparency in annual reports and where the leadership in making those reforms realities should come from.

CHAPTER 11

Modifying Your Game Plan

A New Form of Portfolio Management

Every investor struggles with the question of how to pick stocks. What should you buy and when? What specific fundamental or technical indicators are dependable? How do you know when to sell?

These basic investment questions cannot be addressed by the contents of the annual report. The report is valuable as a first document to review, to locate industries or companies whose stock might belong in your portfolio. But to get a current and updated view of a company's history and status, you need to move beyond the annual report. A benefit of using a research service like the S&P Stock Reports is the uniformity of the information that the report provides for each company under review. Side-by-side comparisons are easy to make. Unfortunately, you cannot get the same historical information from the annual report. Each company provides what it wants to and for a number of years that it determines, without any specific standards or universally agreed-upon format for presentation.

When you compare the uniformity of a research report for a company to the presentation in each company's annual report, the problem becomes clear. Since there is no consistency in how annual reports are formatted or presented, additional information is essential. For many investors, some sections of the annual report are useless. The letter to stockholders is obviously self-serving, in some cases laughably so. The footnotes to the financial statements are so technical that even experienced accountants have trouble understanding them; for most investors, even comprehension of a footnote does not help in determining its applicability to the basic concerns of valuation and profitability.

▲ THE ROLE OF THE ANNUAL REPORT

The perception of the annual report is that it can be used for many purposes, including the selection of stocks to buy, hold, or sell. This perception is misguided. Because the annual report is prepared only annually, it is outdated for much of the year. In fact, even by the time it has been published, the annual report is likely to be three months or more out of date. It becomes historical the moment it is published.

> **Key point:** The annual report and its financial disclosures are outdated by the time you read them. This is why you also need to review all forms of current information that you can find.

For specific and updated financial information, the quarterly SEC filings are more current than the annual report, but even these are not current enough to let you understand the status of a company today. For that, you need to check four things:

1. *Current financial news.* The news can affect not only specific companies, but entire industries as well. If you read, for example, that a trend toward an increasing number of class-action lawsuits against pharmaceutical companies is underway, that fact changes the risk level of *all* companies in that industry. This news is available on investing web sites, through brokerage and trading sites, and from financial magazines, newsletters, and newspapers.

The current news pertaining to a specific company is also important. For example, you might want to buy stock in Krispy Kreme because you like the product and you think the franchise has tremendous growth potential. But unless you kept up with the current news in 2005, you might not have known that the company had missed its financial statement filing deadlines for an entire year.

2. *Earnings reports and forecasts.* Following earnings announcements for companies and for competitors of those companies is one way to remain current. When a company announces earnings that are below forecasts, this could be a red flag. But you should always make an important distinction: The red flag is important when a company announces earnings that are lower than its *own* expectations, but when the earnings fall short of a Wall Street analyst's predictions, it is not as important. A "great game" played in the Wall Street culture is to evaluate companies based on how well their earnings conform to an analyst's predictions, even when those predictions have little or nothing to do with the company's actual financial performance (or the timing of transactions, accounting policies, or seasonal factors). Quarterly earnings reports are given great importance on Wall Street. However, they are not reliable indicators of trends, for several reasons. The first is the obvious seasonal factor (you cannot expect a retail company's sales and earnings to be as high in the first calendar quarter as in the preceding fourth quarter, for example). Second, quarterly results are unaudited. And third, so many internal accounting decisions will affect quarterly results that deciding to buy or sell stock based on those earnings is a potentially expensive mistake.

3. *Stock research services.* A reliable source for information about the current status of companies is an independent research and analysis service. The large Wall Street institutions provide publications to their clients, primarily to promote stock purchases, but the cost of trading through a full-service brokerage can be far higher than the $6 to $20 charged by most discount brokers. Full-commission brokers charge as much as $150 for comparable services, often accompanied by an argument that the research and recommendations you get as part of the package justify the higher cost. But if you are able to find research as a free account service for a lower-cost online trading account, this contradicts the claims of some of the older, more established full-service brokerage firms. The free company research reports are valuable additions to annual and quarterly financial statements and to the annual report.

4. *Current and recent price trends and history.* Although emphasis is properly placed on the fundamentals, the stock's recent and historical trading range is also important. When you see a stock's one-year range acting in a highly volatile manner, you need to find out why. It is often the case that price volatility is accompanied by revenue and earnings volatility. In addition, the more volatile stocks may also have high core earnings adjustments, an indication that changes in accounting policies, high contingencies, and questionable accounting practices may all play a role in the uncertainty. So a company's stock history is not merely a technical signal; it could lead you to a closer examination of its recent financial history as well.

Key point: The historical trading range, P/E ratio, revenues and earnings, and other indicators can help you draw conclusions about companies. But of equal importance is the question: What is going on this week?

▲ MANAGING PUBLIC RELATIONS VERSUS DISCLOSURE

In the wake of the Sarbanes-Oxley Act and massive settlements by companies for misstating their accounting in the past, have things changed? The annual report continues to look the same as it did before reform; if anything is different, footnotes have gotten longer and more technical than ever. This is at least partly due to the need on the part of corporations to disclose as fully as possible. But don't confuse disclosure with transparency. A second change has been the level at which corporations talk about their dedication to transparency, improved corporate governance, and better communication with investors. Unfortunately, few of these commitments have translated into visible improvement in the annual report's format or content.

The very fact that corporations make no distinction between the promotional and factual sections of the annual report tells the whole story. There is little, if any, improvement in transparency. Perhaps one great failure of the SOX legislation is that it did not (and perhaps could not) demand better corporate transparency.

You cannot get everything you need from the annual report. A short list of changes that would go a long way to improving the annual report follows:

1. *Add a footnote disclosing the details of executive compensation.* The corporate scandals involving Enron, WorldCom, Quest, Tyco, and other companies focused a great deal of attention on the conflicts of interest involving executive incentive pay. When executives are compensated based on reported earnings and the stock's price, there is a serious problem, and this situation has not changed. Another problem is the exceptionally high executive pay even in underperforming companies. This means that investors—the *equity owners* of those corporations—are often seeing their equity given to CEOs and other executives, even when those executives' performance doesn't merit it. A study ending in 2004 revealed that for the 60 companies with the worst five-year performance history, $769 billion in net losses were reported, but executive compensation was over $12 billion in the same period.[1]

> **Key point:** It does not make sense that most corporations fail to disclose executive compensation. It makes it look as if they have something to hide . . . and the facts often support that appearance.

2. *Improve reforms of the accounting industry.* Since SOX was passed, little change has been seen in the activities of auditing firms, and problems continue to this day. The problem resides partly with the Public Company Accounting Oversight Board created as part of SOX. It was formed in 2002, but by the end of 2005, it had filed only four disciplinary cases, and those were against very small firms. No cases have been filed against the major firms, even though problems with the audited financial statements of listed companies persist.[2]

> **Key point:** Here's a paradox: Since SOX passed, earnings restatements have doubled each year. At the same time, no disci-

plinary actions have been taken against any of the large national
accounting firms.

3. *Revise the law to more severely penalize companies whose financial
statements are later revised.* The new law was well intended, but it has not
changed the basic reporting problem. In fact, the problem has gotten
worse. Despite the fact that internal accounting is reviewed by auditors
and signed off on by outside firms, earnings restatements in the year 2005
were nearly 50 percent greater than in 2004. The total for 2005 was about
1,200 restatements, compared to 650 in 2004 and only 270 in 2001.[3] One
argument offered to explain this higher number is a higher level of vigi-
lance among auditors. While it is true that accounting rules are complex,
it does not seem reasonable that a greater number of earnings restatements would result from SOX.

Key point: Laws don't always deliver what they promise.
Since SOX was passed, the annual number of earnings restatements has doubled each year.

▲ THE NEED FOR REFORM

Reforms are needed on all fronts, beyond SOX and federal- and state-
level lawsuits against corporations and auditing firms. Investors' difficulty
in interpreting the information in annual reports remains a problem.
Additional reforms are still needed in two areas: annual report formatting
and the accounting industry.

Needed Reforms in Annual Reports

The first type of reform would be relative simple. A *uniformity of sequence
and titles* would ensure that investors would find the same sections of the
annual report in the same order; these sections would have the same titles
would cover the same specific types of information.

A similar reform is needed in footnotes. Creating a *specific sequence and specific titles for footnotes* would clean up what today is a very confusing situation. Every company devises its own sequence and titles. Some companies even exclude certain types of footnotes that are common in other companies' annual reports. There is no standard for the sequence or titling of footnotes, and this is a troubling situation for investors.

Footnotes are presented at the whim of the company, and many types of disclosures are simply not provided. A reform requiring *specific disclosures* should be included so that investors will know in advance what they will find. Examples include comparisons between different types of accounting assumptions (see the next paragraph) and the details of executive compensation. This should include information about a specified number of the highest-paid executives, the types of compensation and the basis for any incentives included, and any pertinent information that would allow you to make judgments about companies based on their compensation policies.

Key point: Annual report reforms would be logical and simple, and would vastly improve the document. Leadership for change should come from the accounting industry, but that is highly unlikely.

A troubling suggestion? Some companies explain executive compensation, but most do not. What is the big secret? Some companies "go public" specifically so that the original founders can cash in their equity, and this is achieved through stock ownership and compensation. Subsequent executives often ensure that their compensation will also be high. The big secret at times may be the belief that if investors were able to see how much executives were being paid, it would look as if they were taking too much stockholders' equity out of the company. That perception could be right.

One of the most important types of reform would create *true* transparency. A new section of the annual report would present *side-by-side formats of accounting results* in three formats. The first would be GAAP (this is what you see now), the second would be the statutory basis (the numbers reported on the company's income tax returns), and the third would be the core earnings (the outcome including only core earnings and excluding nonrecurring items). This is perhaps the most controversial reform suggestion, but why? Accountants and corporate executives know the potentially vast differences among these three formats, and are also aware of the manipulations performed in the accounting system, *all perfectly legal and allowed under GAAP*—but deceptive. The simultaneous presentation of financial statements in different accounting formats would revolutionize reporting and raise many disturbing questions. But it would also make the mysteries of accounting truly transparent for all to see. This is not a new idea. In China, where different reporting standards can be exceptionally confusing, many publicly traded companies present their audited financial statements using three different standards, available for all to compare. These are the International Accounting Standards (IAS; the most conservative), Hong Kong Accounting Standards, and U.S. GAAP, the standard that all listed companies on U.S. stock exchanges use. It is difficult to imagine why anyone would object to a presentation of information in three formats for U.S. companies. It would at the very least enable everyone to see different interpretations of operating results each year.

Another important reform would be a *mandated number of years to include in side-by-side comparisons.* Currently, key financial data and segment information are presented for varying numbers of years. Most companies include at least three years in these presentations. Key data often go out five years, and some companies include ten. But if you want to line up annual reports for two or more companies, you will have trouble finding the same time period for these data.

Finally, a reform would ensure the *specific inclusion of key financial facts.* Today, each company decides which facts to include and which ones to leave out. Some break out operating expenses and operating earnings separately, while others do not. Some provide the current ratio and debt ratio, P/E ratio, and stock trading ranges; others do not. A mandated list of what to include and in what order would help investors and analysts to manage their research. Today, in order to develop histories for several companies, you need to dig into the footnotes or use outside research services. One of the big advantages in referring to the S&P Stock Reports, for example, is their simplicity, the uniformity of the information presented, and the number of years (10) for all facts presented in the financial charts. This suggestion simply proposes that the same uniformity should become a requirement for the annual report.

Needed Reforms to Eliminate Accounting Conflicts of Interest

The ongoing problems in the accounting industry today are as scandalous as the fraud, misrepresentation, and accounting industry's complicity of the past. Higher restatements in 2005 than in preceding years and a lack of disciplinary action by the oversight board are contradictory. If restatements are higher, shouldn't there be more disciplinary action by the regulatory board?

The *rapid reform of GAAP* would go a long way toward correcting the current problem. GAAP is too decentralized and too complex, and it takes too long to fix known problems. For example, even though the noninclusion of stock option expense has been known by the industry for years and by the public since 2002, it took *four years* for the new requirement that companies must report stock option expenses on their financial statements to become "the rule."

> **Key point:** Accounting reform *should* be part of the natural process undertaken by a strong accounting industry. Unfortunately, that industry lacks the resolve to participate in reform. Its recent history has shown resistance to change on all fronts.

A second problem is the highly misleading and inaccurate accounting practices that are allowed under GAAP. Companies can manipulate numbers to create the appearance of strong working capital, higher earnings, and strong revenue trends, even though these practices deceive investors. The GAAP system should go beyond verification of transactions and include a test of the *ethical* practices involved in those accounting decisions. If a practice deceives investors, it should be disallowed—or, at the very least, it should have to be disclosed.

Another reform that would completely eliminate the accounting conflict of interest would be for corporate leadership to *separate audit and*

nonaudit functions. The Sarbanes-Oxley Act included many specific reforms designed to control and even to eliminate conflicts of interest, but
many exceptions were left. Today, accounting firms are still consulting
and earning as much from nonaudit services as from audits. This is a
glaring flaw in what is supposed to be an independent auditing procedure. The solution, though, will be found not in law but in corporate
leadership. If CEOs and CFOs would impose a policy of using separate
accounting firms for audit and nonaudit work, the conflict of interest
would disappear.

> **Key point:** If corporate leaders would simply create a new pol-
> icy of keeping audit and nonaudit work by outside firms sepa-
> rate, this would solve the entire accounting conflict-of-interest
> problem.

Why hasn't this been done? For the most part, corporate leadership
sees advantages in working with a single outside auditing firm. The
amount of consultation payments to firms for nonaudit work has a direct
bearing on how audit work is performed and on the degree to which an
outside firm can be truly independent. This is especially true if and when
the audit team disagrees with the client's interpretation of the accounting
rules. A supporter of the current system might argue that there are sound
management reasons to use the same accounting firm for all consultation,
but the need for true independence should mandate that the outside audit
function be performed by an accounting firm that has no other revenue-
based interest in that client. Some objections have been raised, based on
the claim that using two different firms will add expense. But if the goal
is objectivity of the auditor, this claim sounds hollow. It would be reassuring to investors if the accounting industry would take the lead in this area
and declare that it is a violation of standards for a firm to perform audit
and nonaudit work for the same client. This is a simple idea, and it also
happens to be true and obvious. But no one can expect the accounting
industry to take such a stand.

A final reform—needed because the accounting industry is clearly not
willing to reform itself—is to fix the apparent problems in the accounting
oversight board. Given the continuation of accounting problems (as evi-

denced by the *growing* number of restatements in 2005 over previous years), it is apparent that more disciplinary actions are needed. The nearly complete lack of such actions makes it clear that this board is not performing a real regulatory or supervisory role. This is an SEC problem, and the SEC needs to make changes to ensure that the board begins functioning as an enforcement and regulatory arm.

▲ WHO SHOULD MAKE THESE CHANGES?

Whenever it is suggested that reforms should be made to an industry, determining who should make the changes is always perplexing. The universal "they" is usually assumed to be the responsible party. "They should fix the problem" is an easy assumption, but, in fact, publicly listed corporations and the various groups involved in putting together annual reports represent a complex culture, one that is clearly flawed. Until investors can rely on the annual report as an honest document that presents everything that they need to know, the system will continue to lack transparency and to present misleading, inaccurate, and incomplete information.

> **Key point:** To transform annual reports into transparent, reliable documents, many reforms are needed. These reforms are logical and sensible, but resistance to even simple change is a formidable barrier.

Reforms should be generated by the following five groups:

1. *Stock exchanges* are best equipped to propose and demand changes in annual report formats, inclusion of information, and titles. It is simple. The exchanges need only make the new standards part of their listing requirements. A company would then have to go along if it wanted to continue having its stock listed on that exchange. The New York Stock Exchange (NYSE) composed a highly detailed report of new listing requirements as part of its 2002 report, which ran 174 pages. Its recommendations and requirements formed much of the basis for the Sarbanes-Oxley Act.[4] The same approach could be used to reform annual reports.

2. *Regulators* need to continue enforcing existing laws and, at the same time, look for ways to augment the laws that are on the books. The SEC was taken by surprise and embarrassed by New York state attorney general Eliot Spitzer when, in 2002 and 2003, he aggressively began fining brokerage firms for their abuses. While the SEC moved cautiously, Spitzer spearheaded a settlement of $1.4 billion from 10 of Wall Street's largest firms for various practices (such as recommending stocks to clients even when they knew that they were low quality).[5]

3. *Management* should lead, and part of that includes making firm, even controversial decisions. Removal of accounting firm conflicts of interest would result from setting a policy of refusing to use the same outside firms for audit and nonaudit work. The big question for investors is, Will management ever be willing to take such a bold step?

4. The *accounting industry* is the most perplexing center for reform. Historically, investors have always considered accounting firms as having the highest ethical behavior—as being the investor's watchdog, ready to blow the whistle on corrupt corporate activities. Investors now know that the accounting industry not only is ineffective in this mission, but has been a willing co-conspirator with its own clients and appears clueless concerning its own conflicts of interest—to the extent that the SEC took away its historical self-regulatory role (through creating the oversight board within SOX). But it is not too late. The industry can reform itself by working with clients to truly separate audit and nonaudit consultation, setting higher standards for its own consulting work, and taking steps to make the GAAP system more efficient, streamlined, and responsive to changing needs.

5. Finally, *individual investors* share the responsibility for reforming a flawed system. Silence is consent, and individuals can have a dramatic impact if they express their dissatisfaction to the organizations that can make a difference. The stock exchanges regulate listed companies and have the power to impose listing requirements. The contact web sites for the major stock exchanges are:

NEW YORK STOCK EXCHANGE	WWW.NYSE.COM
NASDAQ	WWW.NASDAQ.COM
PHILADELPHIA STOCK EXCHANGE	WWW.PHLX.COM
AMERICAN STOCK EXCHANGE	WWW.AMEX.COM

Contact information for organizations within the accounting industry is:

Public Company Accounting Oversight Board	www.pcaobus.org
Financial Accounting Standards Board (FASB)	www.fasb.org
American Institute of Certified Public Accountants (AICPA)	www.aicpa.org
Big Four firms:	
Deloitte & Touche	www.deloitte.com
Ernst & Young	www.ey.com
KPMG	www.kpmg.com
PricewaterhouseCoopers	www.pwcglobal.com

Regulatory agencies include:

Securities and Exchange Commission (SEC)	www.sec.gov
National Association of Securities Dealers (NASD)	www.nasd.com
North American Securities Administration Association (NASAA)—use to locate state securities regulators for each state	www.nasaa.org

The task you face in using annual reports is daunting. The fault lies partially with listed companies, which view these documents partially as serving promotional needs and partially as disclosure documents. Sensitivity to the investor's needs is lacking. True transparency is an admirable goal, but corporations have not yet met this goal. The problem is augmented by a flawed accounting industry that, in spite of its assumed role as watchdog, has failed the investing public and continues to resist true reform.

Depending on the stock exchanges to make real change may be the best opportunity to supplement the Sarbanes-Oxley Act. This complex legislation was a good start. Next, federal and state regulators need to again work with the stock exchanges and with corporate leaders to create a better, more accessible, and more straightforward format for the corporate annual report.

Your decisions to buy and hold stock are influenced by the information you receive. In that regard, you rely on what you are told in the annual report. It is frustrating and disturbing that, even after a series of corporate problems involving deception and fraud, today's corporate leaders continue to view the annual report as a device for their own purposes, not for investor interests. The fact that you have to supplement the information in the annual report with other sources for research and analysis is disappointing, but it remains necessary for wise analysis.

Even so, the annual report does provide you with many types of important and valuable information. The insights you gain from the confusing array of technical qualifications and disclosures, and the optimistic promotions offered by the sometimes inane letter to stockholders, can and do serve as a worthwhile starting point in your quest for better information, more consistent profits, and a reliable, dependable, and accurate report.

G L O S S A R Y

accumulated depreciation a negative asset account representing the total of the depreciation claimed each year to date. Total asset cost minus accumulated depreciation equals the book value of fixed assets reported on the balance sheet.

amortization the recognition of an expense over two or more years. Prepaid assets and certain intangible assets are amortized, meaning that the total amount is recognized as an expense over several years rather than in a single year.

audit trail a string of documents and records that can be used to trace transactions from original documents through to the financial statements.

balance sheet one of the three principal financial statements, prepared to report the balances of all asset, liability, and stockholders' equity accounts as of a specific date (year-end or quarter-end in most cases). The other financial statements report transactions over a period of time ending on the same reporting date as the balance sheet.

Big Four the largest accounting firms in terms of both audit and non-audit services. The four firms are PricewaterhouseCoopers, KPMG, Deloitte & Touche, and Ernst & Young. When Arthur Andersen was in existence, the group was called the Big Five, and before mergers, the Big Eight.

bill and hold accounting a procedure in which customers enter into a contract with the company to buy goods in the future, but all or part of the dollar amount of the contract is entered as earned income in the year in which the contract is entered into.

book value per share the calculated net worth of a company divided by the average number of shares of common stock outstanding during the year. The calculation usually excludes all intangible assets.

capital assets assets that are expected to last more than one year; when such items (buildings, equipment, and so on) are acquired, they should be set up as assets and be depreciated over a specified recovery period rather than being written off as expenses in any single year. Also called fixed or long-term assets.

capital stock the issued stock of a company, sold to investors to provide equity capitalization. Stock consists of one or more classes of common and preferred stock, minus any treasury stock (shares that the company has repurchased on the market and retired).

capitalization (1) the process of setting up purchases as assets and depreciating them over many years, rather than writing them off as current-year expenses. (2) A source of funding for a company's operations, with two sources making up total capitalization: debt (long-term liabilities) and equity (stockholders' equity).

cash flow the movement of money into and out of a company. Cash flow is essential for funding ongoing operations and for expansion.

closing the books the process of ending a month, quarter, or year and allowing no further transactions. Accountants usually close the books at or near the end of the period. Any transactions occurring after the books are closed are posted in the following accounting period.

contingent liabilities obligations that might or might not materialize. An actual value for these potential liabilities cannot be calculated, since it is not known whether the contingency will become an actual liability. Typically, contingent liabilities include damages claimed damages in lawsuits that have filed but have not yet been decided.

cookie jar accounting the practice of deferring the recording of some revenues and earnings in exceptionally profitable years and recognizing them in later years. The effect is to smooth out trends and to falsely reflect lower volatility than would be shown if revenues were booked in their proper years.

core earnings those earnings related only to the core business of the company, excluding nonrecurring items, extraordinary items, and the income or loss resulting from changes in accounting policies, and including expenses that occurred but were not reported by the company. The concept was devised by Standard & Poor's Corporation as a means for rating a company's credit and defining an accurate earnings history.

cost of goods sold the sum of all direct costs that are specifically identified as relating to current-period revenues. The difference between revenues and the cost of goods sold is the gross profit (profit before deducting expenses).

current assets and liabilities all assets that are in the form of cash or are convertible to cash within one year (accounts receivable, inventory, notes receivable, and securities), and all liabilities that are payable within the next 12 months (including 12 months' payments of long-term liabilities).

current ratio current assets divided by current liabilities; a popular and important test of working capital. The outcome 2 to 1 (often expressed as 2) is considered a standard for comparison.

debt ratio long-term debt divided by total capitalization (long-term debt plus shareholders' equity); an important test of capitalization. The trend in this ratio reveals whether debt capitalization is growing or shrinking as a percentage of the total.

deferred asset an asset set up to defer the recognition of costs or expenses that were paid early. For example, a company purchases merchandise at the end of December, but the related revenue is not booked until January. A deferred asset is set up at year-end and the payment is recorded, then the entry is reversed and the purchase booked as merchandise purchased the following month.

deferred credits revenue that was received in advance of the period in which it is earned. For example, a customer pays for goods in advance, and the company closes its books. Because the revenue will not be earned until the following period, it is set up as a deferred credit. Once the revenue is earned, the credit is reduced and the payment is booked as current revenue.

depreciation the writing off of capital assets over a prescribed period of years (the "recovery" period). Each year's depreciation expense is offset by an entry to Accumulated Depreciation, which reduces the book value of the capital asset.

disbursements journal an accounting document designed specifically to record all payments made by a company in the form of checks written; the totals are transferred at the end of the month or other period to the general ledger.

disclosure the revelation of a material fact, one that may affect valuation, profitability, or both. Disclosures of all material information are required as part of the footnotes section of the annual report.

dividend yield the percentage earned through dividends, calculated as dividends per share as a percentage of the current stock market price.

dividends declared the value of dividends declared by the board of directors and payable to common shareowners.

double-entry bookkeeping a system of recording transactions in a methodical manner while ensuring that math errors are not made. The system involves entering a debit and a credit for every transaction. For example, revenues are recorded with a debit to either Cash or to the Accounts Receivable asset account and a credit to Revenue. Payments involve debits to various expense accounts and an offsetting credit to Cash. In a properly controlled system, the sum of all debits will always be equal to the sum of all credits.

earned income any income properly booked in the current accounting period, with related costs matched and booked in the same year. When income has been earned but payment has not yet been received, the income is accrued. When payment has been received but income has not yet been earned, the payment is set up as a deferred credit, to be recognized as earned income in a future year.

earnings per share (EPS) the dollar value of total earnings during a fiscal year divided by the average number of common shares of stock outstanding during the same period.

expenses payments for goods and services that are not directly related to revenues; often divided into selling expenses and general and administrate expenses.

exponential moving average (EMA) a type of moving average that gives greater weight to more recent data and less weight to older data.

financial statements three statements required to be presented in annual reports: the balance sheet, the summary of operations, and the statement of cash flows. Together these statements provide valuation, profitability, and cash flow summaries of the organization.

footnotes a section of the annual report in which specific disclosures related to the information on the financial statements are made. This is usually the longest section of the annual report.

fundamental analysis a process of quantifying the value and profit potential of a company based on its financial status and results of operations.

fundamental volatility a concept defining market risk on the basis of consistency of financial results. When revenues and earnings are steady and predictable, investment risk is also low; and when reported results and adjustments (including annual core earnings adjustments) are high, investment risk is also high, as measured by fundamental status.

GAAP (Generally Accepted Accounting Principles) the standards used in the accounting industry to determine the most acceptable and consistent methods to be used in financial reporting.

general journal a journal used in an accounting system for all entries that are not properly included in the receipts journal or the disbursements journals, such as noncash expenses, reversal of prepaid items, error corrections, current-month accruals, and the reversal of the prior month's accrual journal entries.

general ledger the book of final entry, where transactions for each account are entered in summarized form from the journals and balances are calculated and carried forward. The general ledger is used for preparation of a trial balance and financial statements.

going concern qualification an auditor's opinion that a company may be unable to continue as a "going concern," meaning that its ability to remain in business is in jeopardy. Such a serious opinion is normally expressed when a company's liabilities exceed its net worth, or when pending litigation or other threats would prevent the organization from continuing operations.

gross margin gross profit as a percentage of revenues; the margin earned by a company before deducting expenses.

gross profit the amount remaining after cost of goods sold is deducted from revenues.

incentive compensation forms of annual compensation to executives based on performance (profits, stock market value, or both), including payments in the form of company stock, granting of stock options, and bonuses.

incurred expenses those expenses that belong in the current accounting year or month, even if they have not yet been paid. An accrual is set up to recognize current expense and offset that expense with an entry to Accounts Payable, a current liability. When the expense is paid, the Accounts Payable entry is reversed.

intangible assets those assets having no physical existence. The most common types are goodwill, organizational expenses, covenants, and trademarks. Some intangibles are amortized over a number of years, and others remain at their recorded value indefinitely.

inventory turnover the average number of times inventory is replaced per year; a test of inventory efficiency.

journals a company's books of original entry, in which a series of transactions are shown in itemized form; the total for a month or some other period is transferred to a general ledger. There are three primary types of journals: the receipts journal, the disbursements journal, and the general journal.

liquidity the availability of working capital, or the health of a company's cash flow. Tests of liquidity assume a relationship between current assets and the current ratio, but they often ignore the effect of changing long-term debt levels.

long-term assets also called fixed or capital assets, those properties of the company that are expected to last more than one year and whose value is depreciated over a specified recovery period.

long-term commitments obligations of a company that are disclosed only in footnotes and not listed on the balance sheet. They include the liability for employee retirement plans, long-term lease commitments, and certain other contractual obligations.

long-term liabilities all liabilities due and payable *beyond* the next 12 months (the current period). This includes the noncurrent portion of notes and contracts payable and bonds issued.

market value the current actual value of an asset, which often is not the same as net book value. For example, the market value of real estate may be considerably higher than the book value, which is recorded at the original purchase price minus depreciation.

matching principle a basic standard in accounting; it states that revenues and related costs and expenses are to be recognized in the same accounting period, with no deferrals, prepaid entries, or other adjustments being used to control trends or to otherwise distort the results.

moving average a type of average in which a set number of values are used, with the oldest value being dropped off as each newer one is added.

multiple the price/earnings ratio. For example, if today's price is $40 per share and the earnings per share in the latest period was $1.60, then the multiple is 25 (the price expressed as a multiple of EPS).

net income the income earned by the company after all forms of income, costs, and expenses have been included.

net return the percentage of net profit, calculated by dividing net income by total revenues and expressing the result as a percentage.

net worth the value of a company, consisting of the net difference between assets and liabilities; also called stockholders' equity.

off-balance-sheet liabilities any obligations of the company that are not reported on the balance sheet, including undisclosed partnerships or subsidiaries, obligations through contracts, and a company's pension or profit-sharing liability.

operating profit the profit resulting from the deduction of costs and expenses from revenues, but before "other" income and expenses or tax liabilities are included.

opinion letter a letter written by independent auditors expressing their belief in the accuracy and reliability of the books and records as reported; the opinion letter is included in the annual report and is also submitted to the Securities and Exchange Commission (SEC) with the company's annual compliance filing.

other income and expenses types of income and expenses that are not attributable to operations, including interest income and expenses, profit or loss from selling capital assets, and currency exchange income or expense.

P/E ratio a ratio calculated by dividing the stock price by earnings per share, expressed as a single factor; also called the *multiple* of earnings.

percentage of completion (POC) an accounting method used by companies with production processes that last longer than a single year (commonly seen in the aerospace and construction industries). Under POC, a portion of earned revenue and costs is booked each period as a project moves toward completion.

prepaid assets products or services paid for in a single year but applicable to more than one accounting period. For example, a three-year insurance premium paid in advance is amortized at 1/36th per month for the next 36 months.

pro forma profits calculated profits based on estimates rather than on actual values. The Latin means "for the same of form." Pro forma accounting has often been abused by accountants by overstating non-core earnings such as profits on pension assets.

qualified opinion an opinion provided by an independent auditor that expresses reservations about the accuracy or fairness of a company's financial statements.

quick assets ratio (acid test ratio) the current ratio excluding inventory; it is used to calculate cash flow when inventory levels are exceptionally high. This recognizes that inventory is the least liquid of current assets, so the "quick assets" test may be a reliable alternative to calculate working capital trends.

ratio a relationship between two related balances or financial outcomes, usually computed by dividing one by the other. Ratios are a more easily comprehended shorthand representation of larger financial values.

receipts journal a journal designed specifically to record revenues, whether in the form of cash or on account (supported by a subsidiary journal tracking customer charges and payments). The total of all transactions is transferred to the general ledger at the end of the month or other period.

restructuring costs adjustments disclosed by corporations for reducing overhead expenses, usually including the cost of severance packages to terminated employees, closed plants and facilities, and reduced markets.

revenues the gross income of a company; its sales; the top line of the summary of operations, before deducting costs or expenses.

Sarbanes-Oxley Act of 2002 (SOX) a federal law expanding the authority and budget of the Securities and Exchange Commission (SEC), intended to curtail conflicts of interest in several major areas: in accounting firms performing audits of publicly traded companies, in nondisclosures and other abuses by corporate executives, and among securities analysts and their employers.

segment information a section of the annual report breaking down revenues and earnings, and sometimes direct costs, by product lines. Segment information is usually provided for the current period and two
prior fiscal years.

simple average an average of two or more values in a field or related
values. It gives equal weight to all values and is computed by dividing
the sum of all values by the number of values.

source documents the invoices, receipts, vouchers, purchase orders, and
contracts that support and prove the validity of the transactions reflected on the company's financial statements and in its books and
records.

spike in any statistic, an aberrant entry in a field of values. To make an
average more representative of typical outcomes, nonrecurring spikes
are removed from the field before averages are calculated.

statement of cash flows one of the three principal financial statements;
it reports the total of all changes in cash, summarized in three major
sections: operating activities, investing activities, and financing activities. The period covered is a fiscal year or quarter, and the ending
date of the reporting period is the same date as the date of the balance
sheet.

stock options a form of compensation in which executives or other employees are given options to purchase a specified number of shares of
the company's stock at a fixed price per share. If the market price of
shares in the future is greater than the stock option's exercise price,
options can be exercised and sold at a profit.

stockholders' equity the value of investors' interest in the organization,
consisting of the difference between assets and liabilities. Equity consists of common and preferred stock and retained earnings (including
the current year's profit or loss), adjusted for dividends declared and
paid.

subsequent events a section of the annual report disclosing material
changes occurring after the books for the year covered by the annual
report were closed, but before the preparation of the report was completed. For example, settlement of a major lawsuit or the acquisition
or sale of an operating segment would be a significant change from
the status reported as of the end of the fiscal year.

sugar bowling the practice of saving some revenues through deferral and then recognizing those revenues in later years when volume is lower. The effect is to create an artificial appearance of low volatility in revenue and earnings trends.

summary of operations one of the three principal financial statements; it reports the total of all revenues, costs, expenses, and profits for a specific period of time, normally a fiscal year or fiscal quarter. The ending date of this period is the same as the balance sheet date.

tangible book value per share the net worth of a company, excluding intangible assets, divided by the average number of shares of common stock outstanding during the year.

technical analysis a process of timing the purchase or sale of stock based on price per share and short-term pricing trends.

trading range the range between the high and low trading prices of stock over a period of time; it is used to test volatility, with a narrower trading range being an indication of lower volatility, and thus lower market risk.

transparency the availability and clarity of corporate information and disclosures. Effective transparency provides investors with complete information concerning material facts, contingencies and commitments, and accounting policies.

trial balance a worksheet prepared by an accountant at the end of each period in which the balances of all accounts are entered and adjusted by closing journal entries in preparation of the financial statements.

unqualified opinion an opinion provided by an independent auditor that expresses no reservations about the financial statements of a company and that asserts the fairness and completeness of those reports.

volatility a measurement of risk based on the breadth of a trading range. An erratic and highly volatile trading range is a sign of higher market risk, whereas a relatively narrow trading range represents lower market risk.

weighted moving average a type of moving average that gives greater importance to more recent data and less to older data. For example, in a field of six values, the latest entry may be added twice and the sum divided by 7, giving the latest value twice the weight.

NOTES

▲ CHAPTER 1

1. *EBRI Issue Brief*, Employee Benefit Research Institute, November 2005, at www.ebri.org.
2. Michael Shroeder, "SEC List of Accounting-Fraud Probe Grows," *Wall Street Journal*, July 6, 2001.
3. Motorola, 2004 annual report, Note 1, at www.motorola.com.
4. SEC, *Financial Reporting Release No. 1*, Section 101; and AICPA, *Rules of Professional Conduct*, Rule 203.
5. FASB, "FASB Facts," at www.fasb.org/facts.
6. Stephen R. Moehrle, Jennifer A. Reynolds-Moehrle, and Wilbur L. Tomlinson, "Is There a Gap in Your Knowledge of GAAP?" *Financial Analysts Journal*, September/October 2002.
7. AICPA 2000, *The Accounting Review*, October 2000, p. 718.
8. David E. Hardesty, *Corporate Governance and Accounting Under the Sarbanes-Oxley Act of 2002* (New York: Warren, Gorham & Lamont, 2002), p. 119.
9. Sunbeam Corporation, 1997 annual report, at www.sunbeam.com.

▲ CHAPTER 4

1. Merck, 2004 annual report, Note 11, at www.merck.com.
2. General Electric, investor information bulletin, July 31, 2002.
3. Helen Jung, "Microsoft's Stock Option End Shows Change," Associated Press, July 10, 2003.

4. *SFAS No. 123*, issued 2004, at www.fasb.org.
5. Standard & Poor's, www.standardandpoors.com.
6. Annual report information at www.ge.com and www.walmartstores
   .com.
7. Altria, 2002 annual report, at www.altria.com.

▲ CHAPTER 6

1. Altria, 2004 annual report, Note 15, at www.altria.com.
2. Papa John's International, 2004 annual report, Item 7, at www.papa
   johns.com.
3. Marsh & McLennan, 2004 annual report, Note 10, at www.mmc.com.
4. S&P Stock Report, Lucent Technologies, December 2005.
5. Ibid.
6. Mary Ellen Lloyd, "Krispy Kreme Unlikely to Deliver Financials by
   December 15," Dow Jones Newswire, November 28, 2005.

▲ CHAPTER 7

1. Lucent Technologies, 2004 annual report, at www.lucent.com.
2. Lucent Technologies, 2003 annual report, at www.lucent.com.
3. S&P Stock Report, Eastman Kodak, December 2005.
4. Eastman Kodak, 2004 annual report, at www.kodak.com.
5. General Motors, 2004 annual report, at www.gm.com.
6. Altria, 2004 annual report, at www.altria.com.
7. Ibid.
8. "Large Scale Biology Corporation's 2004 Financial Statements Contain Auditor's Qualified Opinion," Market Wire, April 21, 2005.

▲ CHAPTER 8

1. Ken Brown and Ianthe Jeanne Dugan, "Arthur Andersen's Fall From
   Grace Is a Sad Tale of Greed and Miscues," *Wall Street Journal*, June
   7, 2002.

2. Sarbanes-Oxley Act of 2002, Title I, ¶ 4003, Section 101.
3. FASB, "FASB Facts," at www.fasb.org/facts.
4. Harvey Pitt, statement, "Regulation of the Accounting Industry," January 17, 2002.
5. Barry Melancon, address, September 4, 2002, at Yale Graduate School of Management.
6. Ibid.
7. "New York Stock Exchange Corporate Accountability and Listing Standards Committee" report, June 6, 2002.
8. Senate Report 107-205, 2002.
9. Cassell Bryan-Low, "Accounting Firms Are Still Consulting," *Wall Street Journal*, September 23, 2002.
10. New York Stock Exchange (NYSE), 2004 annual report, at www.nyse.com.
11. "What the New Options Rules Mean for Your Pay," *Wall Street Journal*, August 7, 2002.
12. Lucent Technologies, 2004 annual report, at www.lucent.com.
13. S&P Stock Report, Lucent Technologies, December 2005.

▲ CHAPTER 9

1. "Public Warned About Analysts," Associated Press (in *Arizona Republic*), June 29, 2001.
2. Howard Schilit, *Financial Shenanigans* (New York: McGraw-Hill, 2002), p. 140.
3. S&P Stock Report, Motorola, December 2005.
4. S&P Stock Report, Xerox, December 2005.
5. Ibid.
6. Xerox Corporation, 2004 annual report, at www.xerox.com.
7. Helen Jung, "Microsoft's Stock Option End Shows Change," Associated Press, July 10, 2003.
8. "New Options Disclosure Rule in the Works," Reuters, August 15, 2002.
9. S&P Stock Report, Wal-Mart, December 2004.

▲ CHAPTER 11

1. MVC Associates, international study by Mark Van Clieaf and Northwestern University study by Janet Langford Kelly, cited in Stephen Labaton, "Four Years Later, Enron's Shadow Lingers as Change Comes Slowly," *New York Times*, January 5, 2006.
2. Labaton, "Enron's Shadow."
3. Ibid.
4. "New York Stock Exchange Corporate Accountability and Listing Standards Committee" report, June 6, 2002.
5. Andy Serwer, "Wall Street Story: There's a Rumble Between Harvey Pitt and Eliot Spitzer. Is Wall Street Big Enough for the Both of Them?" *Fortune*, July 8, 2002.

INDEX

About the Author

Michael C. Thomsett has written more than 60 books on topics including investments, options, accounting, business, and real estate. Prior to his fulltime writing career, the author was an accountant who worked in the San Francisco Bay Area. He owned and operated his own accounting service for four years and also worked for several insurance companies and a major subsidiary of General Electric, Utah International.

In 1978, Thomsett began writing part-time and also began a consulting company in the financial services industry. His clients included a securities broker-dealer, an insurance master agency, and other financial services firms, such as life insurance and health insurance companies, real estate brokers, and financial planning companies. In 1985, he began writing fulltime and closed his consulting firm.

In 1985 and 1986 Thomsett wrote and published over 500 articles, including sales to *American Way, Consumers Digest, USAir Magazine, Delta Sky, Your Home, Home,* and dozens of professional and trade journals. He also began writing books and has remained a fulltime freelance author to this day. He has published many books with AMACOM and has also written for Wiley, Dearborn, Financial Times, and other major business publishers.

Among his major books are *Getting Started in Options* (Wiley), which has sold over 250,000 copies and as of the printing of this book, is in its 6th edition. The author also has written numerous real estate and business management books over the course of his career.

Thomsett is also a frequent speaker at a variety of trade shows, investment seminars, and other venues. He has appeared as a guest on numerous financial television programs, including CNNfn ("The Money

Gang") and Fox News ("Your World with Neil Cavuto" and "Fox and Friends"). He also has been a guest on hundreds of radio programs.

The author has lived in Washington State since 1989 when he moved from the San Francisco Bay Area. His authorship blog site is http://thomsettpublishing.blogspot.com/